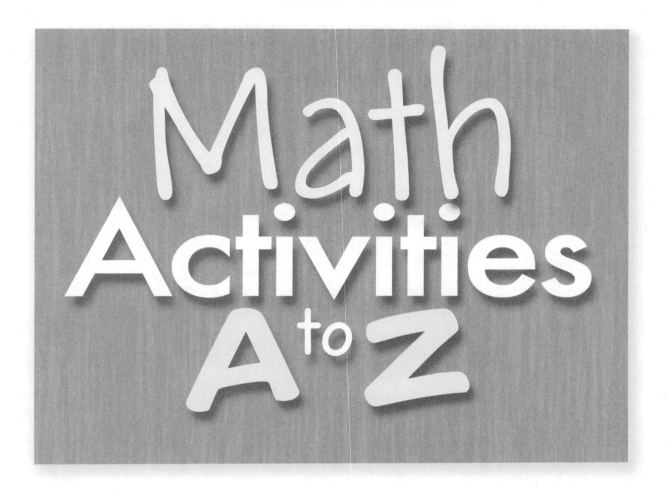

Join us on the web at

EarlyChildEd.delmar.com

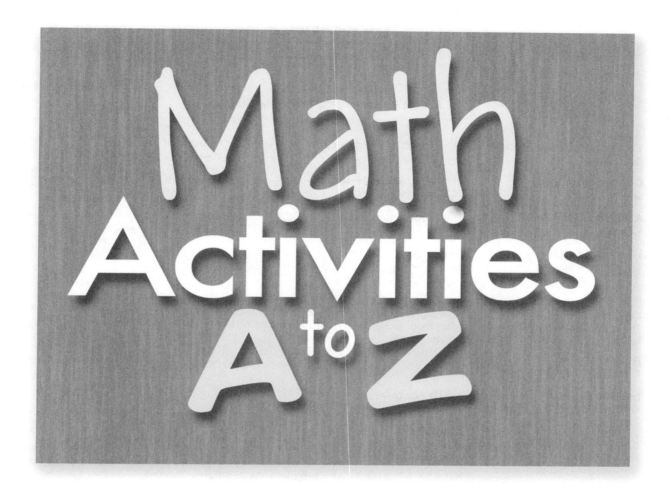

Joanne Matricardi
Jeanne McLarty

THOMSON

DELMAR LEARNING

Australia Canada Mexico Singapore Spain United Kingdom United States

THOMSON

DELMAR LEARNING

Math Activities A to Z
Joanne Matricardi and Jeanne McLarty

Vice President, Career Education SBU:
Dawn Gerrain

Director of Editorial:
Sherry Gomoll

Acquisitions Editor:
Erin O'Connor

Editorial Assistant:
Stephanie Kelly

Director of Production:
Wendy A. Troeger

Production Editor:
Joy Kocsis

Production Assistant:
Angela Iula

Director of Marketing:
Wendy E. Mapstone

Cover Design:
Joseph Villanova

Composition:
Pre-Press Company, Inc.

Library of Congress Cataloging-in-Publication Data

Matricardi, Joanne.
   Math activities A to Z / Joanne Matricardi and Jeanne McLarty.— 1st ed.
      p. cm. — (Activities A to Z series)
   Includes bibliographical references and index.
   ISBN 1-4018-7235-2 (alk. paper)
   1. Mathematics—Study and teaching (Preschool)—Activity programs—United States.   I. Title.
   QA135.6.M387 2005
   372.7—dc22

2004024063

NOTICE TO THE READER

Table of Contents

Preface

Math has become increasingly important in the preschool years. Elementary schools move at such a rapid pace that the first-grade curriculum has been pushed down to kindergarten, and the kindergarten curriculum is now in most four-year-olds' preschool classrooms. Math readiness activities have become commonplace in preschools and child care centers.

The purpose of *Math Activities A to Z* is to provide teachers, parents, and student teachers with a collection of hands-on activities to promote the acquisition of math concepts. Some of the activities may appear repetitious, but children do not learn unless they have the opportunity to practice repeatedly. The activities have been designed to change the materials in order to reinforce necessary concepts.

Many of the lessons presented include the use of patterns in creating materials. All suggested patterns are located in the appendix. The patterns are not meant for one-time use; materials should be carefully created and preserved for future service. The "Helpful Hints" section contains suggestions for material preservation.

The activities are presented in a lesson plan format. Sections included in each activity are "Developmental Goals," "Learning Objective," "Materials," "Adult Preparation," and "Procedures." The "Developmental Goals" are the math concepts to be explored and may also include physical and social considerations. The "Learning Objective" is a behavioral statement of the child's use of certain materials to accomplish the immediate goal of the lesson. The "Materials" section presents all supplies that are required, from preparation through implementation of the activity. The "Procedures" section lists the step-by-step process through which the child can successfully accomplish the lesson.

Additional sections may also be included in the lesson plan. At times, "Variation," "Expansion," and/or "Activity Suggestion" sections are included. "Safety Precautions" are presented when objects used may necessitate closer supervision of the child or children, and "Notes" may provide other useful information.

Teaching children math concepts depends on their developmental abilities, so an appropriate age range for each activity is suggested. Knowing the child's or children's abilities and attention span will help in determining what activities may be done and whether or not those activities need to be altered. At times, the alterations are suggested at the beginning of the activity. In "Acorns and Squirrels," actual acorns are used for ages 3–5. However, it is recommended that acorn patterns be used for 2-year-olds, rather than actual acorns. It is also suggested that only numbers 0–5 be utilized for younger children, or that the children match shapes instead of counting numbers. When number concepts are presented, the average range of numbers for the child to recognize and count is given.

Traditionally, math activities for one-year-olds are very simplified and do not involve specific task assignments, so activities appropriate for a child of this age are not included in this book. Math with toddlers is spontaneous and is accomplished mostly through dialogue ("Please hand me two trucks") and songs (e.g., "Three Little Monkeys Jumping on the Bed"). Two-year-olds are able to count up to their age; as the year progresses and individual differences emerge, numbers up to five should be included. During the third year, a child should be able to count and recognize numbers from 0 to 10. After the child turns four, the numbers 11–20 should be slowly introduced. In our multi-age classroom (ages 2½–4), we have two numbers of the week (such as 4 and 14). We work on the single-digit number with the younger children and focus on the double-digit number for those who are ready.

Math Activities A to Z provides rational counting activities. Children first develop the ability to count by rote, that is, by simply reciting the numbers in order ("1, 2, 3, 4, 5, . . ."). Rational counting, which has also been referred to as true counting, means assigning a number to a set of objects ("There are four apples on the table"). This type of counting is more difficult, and a child's ability to do both must be assessed. Understanding what your child or children know will help you determine your focus.

Most activities in this book list procedures to be carried out by a single child. But the lessons may be used with small groups or with an entire class as well as with individual children. When introducing a new concept, it is best to keep the ratio of children to adults at the lowest rate possible. As children become more adept at the activity, additional children may be included in the activity. Group time is an excellent opportunity for math activities that promote development of large muscles—activities such as "Shoe Matching" or the "Wrapped Box Hunt."

Math Activities A to Z provides two indexes. The "Index of Math Concepts" allows you to find activities that fill a specific need. The "Index of

Units" provides activities to accompany a theme-based curriculum. The way in which you choose to implement the use of math activities in your classroom or home is left to your discretion. Whatever you do, have fun with math. Your enthusiasm will be contagious!

ANCILLARY MATERIAL

ONLINE COMPANION™

The Online Companion™ is an accompaniment to *Math Activities A to Z*. This site contains additional hands-on math activities for young children. The activities are written in the same lesson plan format found in this book. These detailed plans include developmental goals, learning objectives, a list of materials, directions for adult preparation, and a step-by-step procedure for the child. The activities are creative, easy to understand, and simple to implement, either in the preschool classroom or at home.

The *Math Activities A to Z* Online Companion™ also provides links to related preschool sites. These links contain early childhood math games, activity ideas, and sources for math manipulatives and supplies. Please visit www.earlychilded.delmar.com to gain access to this Online Companion™.

ACKNOWLEDGMENTS

This book is an accumulation of original and shared ideas developed over 40 years of teaching young children. Many thanks to our coworkers, students, and their parents for sharing and experimenting with us.

We, and the editors at Thomson Delmar Learning, would also like to thank the following reviewers for their time, effort, and thoughtful contributions which helped to shape the final text:

Patricia Capistron
Rocking Unicorn Preschool
West Chatham, MA

Meredith Chambers, M. Ed.
Truman College
Chicago, IL

Vicki Folds, Ed.D.
Broward Community College
Coconut Creek, FL

Jody Martin
Crème de la Crème
Golden, CO

Judy Rose-Paterson
Childtime Children's Centers
Escondido, CA

Marilyn Rice, M. Ed.
Tuckaway Child Development
Richmond, VA

Michelle Rupiper, Ph.D.
University of Nebraska-Lincoln
Lincoln, NE

Brenda Schin
Child Care Consultant
Ballston Spa, NY

Joanne Matricardi
Jeanne McLarty

HELPFUL HINTS

Through the years, we've developed strategies to make our math activities proceed more efficiently. Many of them deal with the preservation of materials so that they may be used year after year. The following procedures have become routine in our classrooms.

✂ Use rubber cement for gluing; white glue may cause paper to wrinkle.

✂ Laminate all materials made with paper. Laminators are obtainable at a wide range of prices. There is usually one available to fit most schools' budgets. Another option is to visit a school or office supply store where laminating may be done for a set fee.

✂ Use clear, unpatterned contact paper to preserve patterns if you do not have access to a laminator, or create materials from heavy tag board.

✂ Store materials in resealable plastic bags that allow you to see at a glance what is inside.

✂ When making folder games, attach a holder for game pieces on the back of the file folder when making folder games by stapling one side of a resealable plastic bag to the back of the folder.

✂ Use each side of each game piece to illustrate a different concept, to reduce the amount of time you spend creating materials. For example, in preparing for the "Acorns and Squirrels" activity, you may put numbers on one side of each squirrel and then flip it over and put a shape on the other side. These pieces can then be used for identifying and matching shapes as well as for counting and number recognition.

✂ Use open floor space for some activities as an alternative to working at the table.

✂ Use foam egg cartons, ice cube trays, or muffin tins for sorting activities.

SUPPLIES NEEDED

Most early childhood programs operate on a limited budget. Many of the materials we use in this book may be purchased at grocery, hardware, office/school supply, dollar, and discount stores. We provide a shopping list for your convenience. Also included is a family letter for use when requesting recycled and household items.

SHOPPING LIST

Adding machine tape
Adhesive bandage strips
Animal cards
Balance scale with buckets
Balls (assorted sizes)
Barrettes
Basket—12 inch
Beads
Black plastic pot—such as those used at Halloween
Bowls—assorted sizes
Box cutter
Brads
Bucket
Buttons
Calendar and numbers
C-clamp
Cereal
Child-size fishing pole
Clear contact paper
Cloth—checkered to resemble tablecloth
Coins—plastic or real
Colored pencils
Construction paper
Contact paper
Copy paper
Cotton swabs
Counters (bears, dinosaurs, buttons, etc.)
Craft sticks
Crayons
Crepe paper streamers
Cups—foam, paper, or plastic

Dice (large)
Dish soap
Dish towel
Divided plastic silverware tray
Doll with long hair
Dried beans of various types, mixed together
Dried black beans
Dried lima beans (large)
Dry erase markers
Envelopes
Erasers (assorted sizes)
Feathers
Felt
File folders
Fishnet (small, aquarium-type)
Flannel board
Foam shapes
Foil star stickers
Food coloring
Gluestick
Goggles
Gold spray paint
Golf tees
Hammer
Hand drill (small)
Hats—assorted
Heavy string
Hole puncher
Holiday ornaments—unbreakable, plastic
Hook and loop tape
Hot glue gun and glue sticks
Interlocking train set
Jacks and balls
Jelly beans
Jewels—flat on one side

Large bag with shoulder strap
Laundry basket
Liquid watercolors
Lunch-size paper bags
Magnetic strips
Magnets
Markers—broad-tipped, fine-tipped, permanent, washable
Map
Marbles
Masking tape
Measuring cup
Metal cookie sheet
Metal rings—1"
Mixed nuts in shell
Muffin tin
Nails
Needle—sewing
Pails—one quart
Paintbrush
Paper clips—metal
Paper lunch bags
Parquetry blocks
Peanuts in shell
Pens
Pencils
Pictures of baby animals
Pictures of mother animals
Pipe cleaners
Plastic animals
Plastic ants
Plastic apples (small)
Plastic bucket and shovel
Plastic ducks
Plastic eggs
Plastic horses
Plastic numbers
Plastic piggy bank

Plastic spiders
Plastic wiggle eyes
Plates—foam, paper or plastic
Playing cards—two decks
Pom-poms—small, craft item
Poster board
Puff paint
Resealable plastic bags—sandwich and gallon size
Ribbons—assorted colors, lengths, textures
Rubber bands
Rubber cement
Ruler
Sandpaper
Scissors
Sectioned tray
Seeds
Small artificial tree
Smocks
Stethoscope—toy
Solid color plastic placemat
Sponges—yellow
Spoons
Stapler and staples
Tag board
Telephones—toy, cellular, or household
Tempera paint
Thread
Tongs
Tongue depressors
Toothpicks
Towels—assorted sizes
Toy xylophone
U.S. flag
Valentines

Washable ink stamp
  pad
Watermelon seeds
Wax paper

White school glue
White sticky labels
Wood glue
Wooden blocks

Wooden squares—
  five inches
Wrapping paper—
  assorted designs

Yardstick
Yarn
Yo-yos
Zippers

FAMILY LETTER

Dear Family,
Many of the items we use in our math center may be found at home. Please save the following circled items and have your child bring them to school.

Acorns
Barrettes
Berry baskets
Bottle caps
Box lids
Buttons
Cardboard cans with plastic lids
Cereal
Cereal boxes
Cloth
Coffee can lids
Coupons
Egg cartons—foam or cardboards
Empty yogurt containers
Envelopes
Felt
French fry containers (from fast-food restaurants)
Golf tees
Hats—assorted
Holiday ornaments
Ice cube trays
Keys
Large shoulder bag
Leaves
Magazines
Milk caps

Muffin tin
Neckties
Newspapers
Park maps
Pennies
Photos of children
Photos of family
Photos of men
Pizza boxes
Plastic cans with lids
Plastic eggs
Real estate booklets
Ribbons
Rocks
Shoe boxes
Silverware
Small empty boxes
Small empty containers
Solid color plastic placemat
Telephones
Tennis cans with lids
Toy xylophone
Wallpaper
Wrapping paper—assorted designs
Yarn
Yo-yos
Zippers

Thanks for your help!

Sincerely,

Acorns and Squirrels

ADULT PREPARATION:

1. Cut out one squirrel for each number, using squirrel pattern and brown construction paper.
2. Write numbers on the squirrels, using a permanent marker. For younger children, put dots on the squirrel equal to the number.
3. Gather acorns.
4. Place squirrels on table in random order.

PROCEDURES:

The child will complete the following steps:

1. Identify the number on each squirrel.
2. Count out acorns equal to the number on each squirrel.
3. "Feed" the acorns to the squirrel.

Note: If acorns are not available, use an acorn pattern to make some (Appendix A2).

VARIATION:

Have the child arrange the squirrels in numerical order.

⚠ SAFETY PRECAUTION:

Acorns may present a choking hazard. Supervise children closely at all times.

AGES: 3–5

AGE: 2 (use acorn pattern, numbers 0–5, or matching shapes)

DEVELOPMENTAL GOALS:

- ✂ To recognize numbers
- ✂ To practice rational counting

LEARNING OBJECTIVE:

Using acorns and squirrel patterns, the child will recognize numbers and count objects.

MATERIALS:

Squirrel pattern (Appendix A1)
Acorns or acorn pattern (Appendix A2)
Brown construction paper
Scissors
Permanent marker

1

Alligators

AGES: 4–5 (may be made suitable for age 2 by simply having the child sort alligators by color)

DEVELOPMENTAL GOALS:

- ✂ To develop an understanding of sets
- ✂ To practice patterning
- ✂ To recognize colors

LEARNING OBJECTIVE:

Using alligators of different colors, the child will recognize colors, sets, and begin to understand patterning.

MATERIALS:

Alligator pattern (Appendix A3)
Construction paper in different colors
Scissors

ADULT PREPARATION:

1. Cut alligators from construction paper, using alligator pattern—at least 10 alligators for each color used.
2. Lay alligators on the table in random order. To introduce patterning, use just two colors. As the children grasp the concept, more colors may be added.

PROCEDURES:

1. Child identifies the colors.
2. Child sorts the colors into sets, such as the green set and the blue set.
3. Adult starts an AB pattern for the child by laying out one green alligator, followed by one blue alligator, then another green alligator, then another blue alligator.
4. Adult helps the child identify the pattern, "Green, blue, green, blue."
5. Adult asks, "What comes next?"
6. Child then continues the AB pattern.

Ants at a Picnic

ADULT PREPARATION:

1. Cut checkered cloth into 4" squares.
2. Write numbers on each of the mini tablecloths.
3. Using the ant pattern and construction paper, cut out ants.
4. Write numbers on the ants to match the numbers on the table-cloths.
5. Place numbered mini tablecloths on table.
6. Set ants on the table on a plate.

PROCEDURES:

The child will complete the following steps:
1. Identify numbers on the tablecloths.
2. Select an ant and identify the number.
3. Match numbered ant to numbered cloth.

EXPANSION:

For younger children, use cloths of different colors to match the colors of the ants.

AGES: 3–5

**AGE: 2
(numbers 0–5)**

DEVELOPMENTAL GOALS:
- ✄ To recognize numbers
- ✄ To match numbers

LEARNING OBJECTIVE:
Using checkered cloth and ant patterns, the child will match numbers.

MATERIALS:
Ant pattern
  (Appendix A4)
Construction paper
Checkered cloth
Permanent marker
Scissors
Plate

Apple Counting

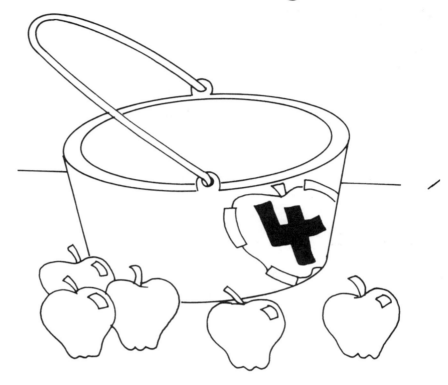

AGES: 3–5

AGE: 2
(numbers 0–5, use plastic apples)

DEVELOPMENTAL GOALS:

- ✄ To recognize numbers
- ✄ To acquire rational counting skills

LEARNING OBJECTIVE:

Using small pails and apples, the child will recognize numbers and count objects.

MATERIALS:

Small pails (found in craft stores)
Small apple-shaped erasers or plastic apples
Foam or plastic plate
Construction paper
Masking tape
Permanent marker
Scissors

ADULT PREPARATION:

1. Cut apple shapes out of construction paper. Apples need to fit into the pail.
2. Write numbers on the apple shape.
3. Tape one numbered apple shape on each pail.
4. Place apple-shaped erasers or plastic apples on a plate on the table.

PROCEDURES:

The child will complete the following steps:

1. Identify the numbers on the pails.
2. Count out the number of apples to match the number on the pail.
3. Place the apples in the pail.

⚠ SAFETY PRECAUTION:

Close supervision of younger children is required when using small erasers, which may present a choking hazard.

4

Apple Matching

ADULT PREPARATION:

1. Cut two apples from each color of felt.
2. Draw matching shapes on each pair of apples (e.g., triangles on green apples, squares on red apples, diamonds on blue apples).
3. Place flannel board on the table or floor.
4. Place felt apples in a bowl beside the flannel board.

PROCEDURES:

The child will complete the following steps:
1. Select an apple from the bowl.
2. Identify the color of the apple and the shape drawn on it.
3. Place the apple on the flannel board.
4. Find the matching apple in the bowl.
5. Place the matching apple on the flannel board.
6. Repeat steps 1–5 until all the apples are matched.

Note: Adults may start the activity for the child by placing one of each color/shape apple on the flannel board. Child then finds the other apple in each pair and places it on the board beside its match.

Copyright © 2005, Thomson Delmar Learning

AGES: 2–5

DEVELOPMENTAL GOALS:

- ✂ To enhance classification skills
- ✂ To recognize colors
- ✂ To recognize shapes

LEARNING OBJECTIVE:

Using a flannel board and apple shapes made of felt, the child will recognize and match colors.

MATERIALS:

Flannel board
Felt in different colors
Scissors
Permanent marker
Apple pattern
   (Appendix A5)
Bowl

Ball Sequencing

AGES: 2–5

DEVELOPMENTAL GOALS:

- ✄ To recognize objects as small or large
- ✄ To sequence objects by size

LEARNING OBJECTIVE:

Using assorted sizes of balls, the child will sequence objects by size.

MATERIALS:

Balls in assorted sizes

ADULT PREPARATION:

1. If the center does not have a variety of balls, write a note home to families requesting that each child bring in his or her favorite ball. Ask each family to put masking tape on their child's ball and write the child's name on it.

PROCEDURES:

1. Adult sets balls on floor.
2. Children identify the smallest ball. Put that ball on the children's left.
3. Tell children, "Look at the balls that are left. Which one is the smallest?"
4. Children select the next size ball and place it to the right of the first ball.
5. Continue steps 2–4 until all the balls have been arranged from smallest to largest.
6. Ask the children:
   a. "Which ball is the largest?"
   b. "Which ball is the smallest?"
   c. "Are any balls the same size?" If the answer is yes, ask, "Which ones?"

Bananas and Banana Tree Folder Game

ADULT PREPARATION:

1. Using construction paper and patterns, cut 11 banana treetops out of green paper; cut 11 tree trunks out of brown paper; and cut 10 variously sized banana bunches out of yellow paper.
2. Using rubber cement, glue the treetops and trunks together.
3. Number the trees from 0–10, using a permanent marker.
4. Glue the trees to the inside of the folder.
5. Staple the resealable plastic bag to the back of the folder (see "Helpful Hints," page xi).
6. Open the folder game on the table.
7. Lay the banana bunch pieces on the table.

PROCEDURES:

The child will complete the following steps:

1. Identify the number on each banana tree.
2. Identify the number of bananas in each bunch and place it on the tree marked with the corresponding number.

Note: Two folders may be needed when gluing trees bearing numbers 0–10, unless the folder is large enough so that the trees don't look crowded.

VARIATION:

Instead of a banana tree, use an apple tree, an orange tree, or a holiday tree with lights.

AGES: 3–5

AGE: 2 (make the folder using only five banana trees, numbered 1–5, and the corresponding number of five banana bunches)

DEVELOPMENTAL GOALS:

- ✄ To recognize numbers
- ✄ To improve rational counting skills

LEARNING OBJECTIVE:

Using construction paper banana bunches and banana trees, the child will recognize numbers and count objects.

MATERIALS:

Banana tree and banana bunch patterns (Appendix A6)
Yellow, brown, and green construction paper
Scissors
File folder
Sandwich size resealable bag
Stapler
Rubber cement
Permanent marker

Barrette Matching

AGES: 3–5

DEVELOPMENTAL GOALS:

✂ To identify colors

✂ To improve matching skills

LEARNING OBJECTIVE:

Using assorted barrettes and a doll, the child will recognize and match colors.

MATERIALS:

Assorted barrettes
Doll with hair, or
  mannequin head

ADULT PREPARATION:

1. Place the doll or mannequin head on the table.
2. Place the barrettes on the table in random order.

PROCEDURES:

The child will complete the following steps:

1. Identify the colors of barrettes on the table.
2. Arrange barrettes in matching pairs.
3. Clip barrettes into the doll's hair, placing matching barrettes next to each other.

VARIATION:

Select 12" lengths of ribbon to match the barrettes and have the child match barrettes to ribbons, clipping barrettes onto ribbons of the same color.

Bead Patterning Bracelet

ADULT PREPARATION:

1. Place beads in two bowls, sorted by color.
2. Start an AB pattern by putting four beads on a pipe cleaner (e.g., red, blue, red, blue).
3. Bend the end of the pipe cleaner up, making a fishhook (to keep the beads from sliding off).
4. Start one bead pattern for each child.

PROCEDURES:

The child will complete the following steps:
1. Identify the colors of the beads on the pipe cleaner.
2. Continue the AB pattern when asked, "What color comes next?"

Note: When the child has finished stringing beads, the pipe cleaner may be twisted into a bracelet.

⚠ SAFETY PRECAUTION:

If the wire at the ends of the pipe cleaner is sharp, cover it with masking tape.

AGES: 3–5

DEVELOPMENTAL GOALS:

✂ To improve patterning skills

✂ To recognize colors

LEARNING OBJECTIVE:

Using assorted beads and pipe cleaners, the child will create a bracelet in AB pattern format.

MATERIALS:

Beads of two different colors

Bowls (one for each bead color)

Pipe cleaners (12" length)

9

B

DEVELOPMENTAL GOALS:
- ✄ To acquire skill in sorting
- ✄ To identify sets

LEARNING OBJECTIVE:
Using dried beans and small containers, the child will sort and match beans into sets.

MATERIALS:
Dried beans of various types, mixed together
Tray with several compartments, or several small plates or bowls
Large bowl

Bean Classification

ADULT PREPARATION:

1. Place one bean of each kind in separate compartments or containers.
2. Pour remaining beans into large bowl.

PROCEDURES:

The child will complete the following steps:
1. Select bean from the large bowl.
2. Place bean in the small bowl or compartment that holds that type of bean.

EXPANSION:

Have the child count the beans in each set.

VARIATION:

Draw lines on paper, dividing it into squares. Glue or draw a different style of bean in each square. Then have the child glue matching beans into the squares.

⚠ SAFETY PRECAUTION:
Beans may be a choking hazard in small children. Supervise the activity closely.

10

3 1833 04761 5965

Bears in a Box

AGES: 3–5

**AGE: 2
(matching bear
size to box size)**

DEVELOPMENTAL GOALS:

✄ Develop spatial concepts

✄ To sequence by size

LEARNING OBJECTIVE:

Using bears and boxes, the child will identify objects as small, medium, and large, and will follow directions regarding spatial placement.

MATERIALS:

Bears of assorted sizes
Boxes of assorted sizes
Masking tape
Permanent marker

ADULT PREPARATION:

1. Ask several parents to send in assorted size boxes.
2. Ask the children to bring in their favorite stuffed bears.
3. Label each bear by writing the owner's name on masking tape and placing it on the bear. (Provide extra bears for those who forget.)
4. Place three boxes of varying sizes on the table.

PROCEDURES:

1. Ask the child, "Which is the largest box?"
2. Ask the child, "Which is the smallest box?"
3. Ask the child, "Which is the middle-sized box?"
4. Ask child to arrange the boxes in order from smallest to largest.
5. Ask the child to identify his or her bears as small, medium, or large.
6. Each child should put his or her bear in the corresponding size box.
7. Practice spatial concepts by giving the children directions to place their bears above, under, beside, between, behind, or in front of the box.

11

B

Bees in the Beehive

AGES: 3–5

AGE: 2
(numbers 0–5)

DEVELOPMENTAL GOALS:

- ✂ To recognize numbers
- ✂ To acquire rational counting skills

LEARNING OBJECTIVE:

Using bee and beehive patterns, the child will identify numbers and count objects.

MATERIALS:

Beehive and bee patterns (Appendix A7)
Yellow paper
Washable markers
Scissors

ADULT PREPARATION:

1. Using the patterns, trace bees and beehives on yellow paper.
2. Cut out bees and beehives.
3. Draw black stripes on the bodies of the bees with a marker.
4. Write numbers on the beehives, starting with the number zero.
5. Lay the beehives on the table in random order.
6. Place the bees in a stack on the table.

PROCEDURES:

The child will complete the following steps:

1. Identify the numbers on the beehives.
2. Place the beehives in order, beginning with the one that is numbered zero.
3. Identify the number on one beehive.
4. Count out that many bees and place them on that beehive.
5. Repeat steps 3–4 with other beehives.

Birds in a Nest

ADULT PREPARATION:

1. Using the patterns and scissors, cut a matching bird and nest out of each style of wallpaper.
2. Lay the nests on the table.
3. Put the birds in a stack on the table or floor.

PROCEDURES:

The child will complete the following steps:

1. Identify the dominant color or design (e.g., stripes, dots) of each nest.
2. Match each bird to its own wallpaper nest.

AGES: 2–5

DEVELOPMENTAL GOALS:

- ✂ To acquire skill in matching
- ✂ To recognize colors

LEARNING OBJECTIVE:

Using bird and nest patterns, the child will identify objects that are the same.

MATERIALS:

Bird and nest patterns (Appendix A8)
Wallpaper in several different designs
Scissors

C

DEVELOPMENTAL GOALS:

- ✂ To count by rote
- ✂ To recognize numbers
- ✂ To expand vocabulary

LEARNING OBJECTIVE:

Using the calendar and numbers, the child will recognize, identify, and count the numbers on the calendar.

MATERIALS:

Calendar
Detachable numbers
Hook and loop tape (to place on numbers and calendar)

Calendar

ADULT PREPARATION:

1. Purchase or create a calendar with detachable numbers. The calendar should be placed on the wall at a child's eye level or hung on a chart stand.
2. Place the appropriate month on the calendar.
3. Label the calendar with the days of the week (do not use abbreviations).
4. Place numbers on the calendar in the appropriate spaces, numbering only those days that have already occurred (e.g., If it is May 3rd, put only the 1 and 2 on the calendar).

PROCEDURES:

1. Ask the child, "What month is this?" If the child does not give the appropriate response, state the correct name of the month.
2. Say, "Yesterday was [Tuesday]; what day is today?"
3. Listen to the child's response. If it is incorrect, state the correct name of the day.
4. Say, "Yesterday was the [10th]; what number is today?"
5. When the child identifies the number that comes after [10], ask the child to count to [11].
6. Instruct the child to jump, clap, or stomp (or some other large muscle activity) with each count.
7. Count and jump, clap, or stomp with the child.
8. Ask the child to identify the number of today's date among the detached numbers. Have the child put that number on the appropriate space on the calendar.
9. End with the child repeating the day, month, and date (e.g., "Today is Thursday, April 5").

14

Cereal Box Matching

ADULT PREPARATION:

1. Use the family letter to request that children bring in empty cereal boxes.
2. Save and collect the boxes to assure that most boxes have duplicates.
3. Lay one of each kind of cereal box in a row on the floor.
4. Place the remaining (matching) boxes on a table or the floor.

PROCEDURES:

1. Sit on the floor with the children, facing the boxes.
2. Start with the box on the far left.
3. Ask the children to identify the cereal. If they give an incorrect response, tell them the name of the cereal.
4. Ask a child to find an identical box on the table. Explain that the box may be smaller or larger, but that it will have the same writing and design.
5. Have the child put the matching box beside its mate on the floor.
6. Proceed with the remaining boxes in left-to-right progression.

Notes: If storage is a problem, cut and use only the fronts of the boxes, which may be stored in a resealable bag or file folder.

If you have difficulty getting duplicate boxes, you may use the copy machine to make one copy of the front of the boxes. This will not violate copyright agreements if they are used only once and used for educational purposes. This falls under the *Fair Use Act.*

AGES: 2–5

DEVELOPMENTAL GOALS:

✄ To improve matching skills

✄ To become familiar with left-to-right progression

LEARNING OBJECTIVE:

Using cereal boxes, the child will identify and match objects that are the same.

MATERIALS:

Cereal boxes
Family letter

Cereal Sorting

DEVELOPMENTAL GOALS:

- ✖ To increase classification skills through sorting
- ✖ To recognize colors

LEARNING OBJECTIVE:

Using cereal, the child will classify objects by matching colors and shapes.

MATERIALS:

Assorted kinds of cereal of different colors and shapes
Plate
Small bowls

ADULT PREPARATION:

1. Pour a mixture of different kinds of cereal on a plate.
2. Set out one bowl for each kind of cereal.

PROCEDURES:

The child will complete the following steps:
1. Identify pieces of cereal by shape and color.
2. Sort cereal into different bowls, one piece at a time.

Note: If children are to eat the cereal at snack time, make sure each child has his or her own plate of cereal and that children wash their hands with soap before beginning the activity.

EXPANSION:

Have the child count and graph the types of cereal in a bar graph fashion (e.g., make vertical columns of the cereal).

Chicken and Eggs

ADULT PREPARATION:

1. Using chicken pattern, trace and cut out 10 chickens.
2. Using egg pattern, trace and cut out 10 eggs.
3. Using markers, decorate the chickens and eggs.

PROCEDURES:

1. Hold up one of the egg cutouts. Ask the child, "What shape is this?"
2. If the child does not respond "oval," state the correct answer.
3. Ask the child to lay the 10 chickens on the table.
4. Ask the child to deliver one egg to each chicken.
5. Have the child count the number of eggs and chickens when finished.

EXPANSIONS:

Have older children create an AB pattern by laying out chicken, egg, chicken, egg, etc.

Promote matching through color or shape recognition by decorating the eggs and chickens in pairs (i.e., red chicken and red egg or chicken with triangles and egg with triangles).

AGES: 2–5

AGES: 3¹/₂–5 patterning

DEVELOPMENTAL GOALS:

- ✂ To use the concept of one-to-one correspondence
- ✂ To recognize the oval shape

LEARNING OBJECTIVE:

Using paper chickens and eggs, the child will place one egg to each chicken.

MATERIALS:

Chicken and egg patterns (Appendix A9)
Paper
Markers
Scissors

C

DEVELOPMENTAL GOALS:

✄ To recognize shapes

✄ To acquire classification skills

LEARNING OBJECTIVES:

Using clown collar and shape cutouts, the children will recognize and match identical shapes.

MATERIALS:

Clown collar pattern (Appendix A10)
Construction paper
Scissors
Glue
Resealable plastic bags
Tape

Clown Shape Collars

ADULT PREPARATION:

1. Trace pattern and cut out a clown collar for each child.
2. Cut out two identical sets of shapes for each child. A set consists of one of each of the following: oval, circle, triangle, rectangle, square, and diamond.
3. Glue one set of shapes on each clown collar.
4. Put the second set of shapes into separate resealable plastic bags, grouping them to match the shapes that are glued onto each collar (one bag of matching shapes per collar).

PROCEDURES:

1. Give each child a clown collar with its bag of matching shapes.
2. The child will lay the collar on the table.
3. Ask the children to select a circle from their bags.
4. Tell the children to find the identical circle on their collars.
5. Each child will place the circle from the bag on top of the matching circle on his or her collar.
6. Repeat steps 2–4 with all shapes until the children's bags are empty.
7. Ask the children to take all of the squares off their collars and put them back into their bags.
8. Repeat step 6 with other shapes.
9. Optional: Allow the children to wear their clown collars by taping the ends of each child's collar together around his or her neck.

Note: Children may do step 3 of "Adult Preparation," but make sure the glue is dry before attempting the matching activity.

18

Coupon Matching

ADULT PREPARATION:

1. Ask parents to send in coupons from the newspaper, magazines or mail.
2. Cut the construction paper into pieces that are the same sizes as the coupons.
3. Cut out the coupons and glue them on the pieces of construction paper.
4. Allow the coupons and construction paper to dry.
5. Make sure that you have at least two of each coupon.
6. Lay one coupon from each set of matching coupons on the table.
7. Put the remaining coupons in a stack.

PROCEDURES:

The child will complete the following steps:

1. Identify the products pictured on the coupons that are laid out on the table (with adult assistance, if necessary).
2. Select one coupon from the stack.
3. Attempt to identify the product pictured on the coupon.
4. Find the matching coupon on the table and place the coupon from the stack on top of it.
5. Repeat steps 2–4 until all cards in the stack have been matched to cards on the table.

EXPANSION:

Sort the coupons into types such as foods, cleaning products, restaurants, etc.

AGES: 3–5

AGE: 2 (using familiar product coupons)

DEVELOPMENTAL GOALS:

✂ To acquire classification skills

✂ To distinguish between same and different

LEARNING OBJECTIVE:

Using coupons, the children will match objects that are the same.

MATERIALS:

Coupons from the newspaper, magazines, or mail
Construction paper
Scissors
Glue

19

Cracker Placemat

DEVELOPMENTAL GOALS:

✂ To improve matching skills

✂ To recognize shapes

LEARNING OBJECTIVES:

Using a placemat and crackers, the child will recognize shapes and match objects.

MATERIALS:

Solid-color plastic placemat (or 9" by 12" construction paper)
Permanent markers
Crackers of varying shapes
Bowls
Laminator and laminating film (or clear contact paper)

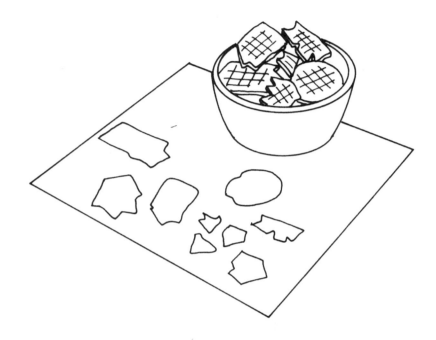

ADULT PREPARATION:

1. Create a shape placemat for each child, using solid-color plastic placemats or construction paper.

2. Select one or two boxes of assorted-shape crackers.

3. Trace one of each cracker shape onto each placemat or piece of construction paper, using a permanent marker. (If using construction paper, laminate it or cover it with clear contact paper.)

4. Wipe off the placemats before setting them on the table.

5. Put crackers in a bowl for each child.

6. Set a bowl of crackers at each placemat.

PROCEDURES:

The child will complete the following steps:

1. Wash hands with soap and water.

2. Identify the shapes on the placemat.

continued

Cracker Placemat continued

3. Select a shape from the bowl and set it on the identical shape on the placemat.

4. Repeat until all crackers are out of the bowl and on the appropriate shapes on the placemat.

Note: When all the shapes have been correctly matched, the child may eat the crackers.

Dad Matching

DEVELOPMENTAL GOALS:

- ✂ To improve classification skills
- ✂ To discern whether objects are the same or different

LEARNING OBJECTIVE:

Using duplicate photographs of fathers, the child will match pictures.

MATERIALS:

Photograph of each child's father or significant male figure
Scissors
Glue
File folders
Copy machine
Paper

ADULT PREPARATION:

1. Ask each child to bring in a picture of his or her father or other significant male figure.
2. Make two copies of each photograph. The original may be returned to the family.
3. Glue one copy of each male figure onto the inside of a file folder. Use more than one folder if all of the photos will not fit on one.
4. Allow the folder(s) to dry.
5. Put the second set of copied photos in a resealable plastic bag or bags and paperclip each bag to the folder that contains matching father figures.

PROCEDURES:

The children will complete the following steps:
1. Take the matching pictures out of the resealable plastic bag.
2. Match the pictures to those pasted in the folder.

Note: Review the children's family histories before starting this activity. If a child does not have a father, the activity may be changed to "Family Matching," or pictures of men may be cut out of newspapers or magazines and photocopied for use in the activity.

Dalmatian and Spots

ADULT PREPARATION:

1. Trace Dalmatian pattern onto white poster board and cut out eleven Dalmatians.
2. Using a permanent marker, write a number (starting with zero) on the back of each Dalmatian. Make sure the marker doesn't show through on the other side.
3. On the right side of each Dalmatian, draw spots corresponding to the number on the back. (If the number is one, make one spot on the front.)
4. Trace fire hydrant pattern on red construction paper and cut out eleven fire hydrants.
5. Write a number on each fire hydrant, starting with zero.
6. Lay the fire hydrants on the table in random order.

PROCEDURES:

The child will complete the following steps:

1. Identify the number on a fire hydrant.
2. Match that fire hydrant to the appropriate Dalmatian by counting the spots on the Dalmatian. (The pure white Dalmatian—no spots—matches the hydrant marked zero.)
3. Continue counting the spots on Dalmatians and matching them with fire hydrants, placing each dog on the hydrant with the matching number.

Note: This activity is self-checking. The child may turn each dog over, revealing the number on its back and then check to see if the numbers on the hydrant and the Dalmatian are the same.

AGES: 3–5

**AGE: 2
(numbers 0–5)**

DEVELOPMENTAL GOALS:

- ✂ To recognize numbers
- ✂ To acquire rational counting skills

LEARNING OBJECTIVE:

Using Dalmatian and fire hydrants, the child will count and identify numbers.

MATERIALS:

Dalmatian and fire hydrant patterns (Appendix A11)
White poster board or tag board
Red construction paper
Permanent marker
Scissors

23

Dice

AGES: 3–5

DEVELOPMENTAL GOALS:

- ✄ To use rational counting
- ✄ To recognize numbers

LEARNING OBJECTIVE:

Using dice and numbered squares, the child will count the spots and match the number of spots to the appropriate numeral.

MATERIALS:

Large dice
Construction paper
Scissors
Marker
Tongue depressors
Stapler

ADULT PREPARATION:

1. Cut construction paper into squares.
2. Write numerals 1–6 on the squares.
3. Staple a tongue depressor to each square, creating a small numbered sign.
4. Lay the numbered signs on the table in random order.

PROCEDURES:

1. The child will roll a single die.
2. The child will then count the dots on the top side of the die.
3. Next the child will hold up the numbered square that represents the number of dots on the die.
4. Repeat steps 1–3.

⚠ SAFETY PRECAUTION:

Supervise young children closely when using small objects, such as dice, to prevent choking hazards.

Doctor's Bag Matching

ADULT PREPARATION:

1. Trace pattern and cut doctor's bag out of black construction paper.
2. Trace and cut tongue depressor, stethoscope, adhesive bandages, and cotton swabs out of white construction paper, then do the same with red construction paper, creating two sets of medical item silhouettes (one red and one white).
3. Glue white silhouettes of medical equipment on the black bag cutout.
4. If possible, laminate all pieces or cover with clear contact paper for durability.
5. Place the red silhouettes in a resealable plastic bag.
6. Place the red pieces resembling medical equipment on the table.
7. Place the real tongue depressor, stethoscope, bandage strips, and cotton swabs on the table.

PROCEDURES:

1. Ask the child to identify the following items on the table: tongue depressor, stethoscope, bandage strips, and cotton swabs.
2. Ask the child to find the similar paper cutouts and to identify each.
3. Ask the child to identify the cutouts on the doctor's bag.
4. The child will place the red silhouette on the same shape on the doctor's bag.
5. Repeat until all red shapes are matched to the white shapes on the doctor's bag.

AGES: 2–5

DEVELOPMENTAL GOALS:

- ✂ To differentiate between same and different
- ✂ To improve classification skills

LEARNING OBJECTIVE:

Using a construction paper "doctor's bag" and paper pieces resembling medical items, the child will match identical objects.

MATERIALS:

Doctor's bag pattern (Appendix A12)
Construction paper
Tongue depressor
Stethoscope—toy
Adhesive bandage strips
Cotton swabs
Scissors
Pencil or pen for tracing
Laminator and laminating film or clear contact paper

25

AGES: 3–5

**AGE: 2
(numbers 0–5)**

**DEVELOPMENTAL
GOALS:**

✂ To use rational
counting

✂ To recognize
numbers

**LEARNING
OBJECTIVE:**

Using construction
paper dogs and bones,
the child will recognize
numbers and count
objects.

MATERIALS:

Dog and bone patterns
(Appendix A13)
Construction paper
Marker
Scissors

Dogs and Bones Counting

ADULT PREPARATION:

1. Trace dog and bone patterns on construction paper and cut out eleven of each.
2. Write numbers, starting with zero, on the dogs.
3. Make dots on the bones to correspond with the numbers.
4. Lay the dogs on the table in random order.
5. Lay the bones on the table in a stack.

PROCEDURES:

The child will complete the following steps:

1. Identify the number on each dog.
2. Select a bone from the stack.
3. Count the dots on the bone and place the bone on the dog with the corresponding number.

Note: Cut one dog and one bone out of the same color construction paper. This makes the activity self-checking.

EXPANSION:

Have the child arrange the dogs in numerical order, starting with zero and using a left-to-right progression.

VARIATION:

Instead of bone patterns, use small dog biscuits. Have the child identify the number on the dog and then "feed" the dog that many biscuits.

26

Duck Pond

AGES: 3–5

AGE: 2 (numbers 0–5, or by having the child identify color of a geometric shape on the bottom of the duck)

DEVELOPMENTAL GOALS:

- ✂ To recognize numbers
- ✂ To improve rote counting skills

LEARNING OBJECTIVE:

Using numbered ducks, the child will identify numbers and will count by rote.

MATERIALS:

Eleven plastic ducks
Permanent marker
Container
Water
Towels for spills

ADULT PREPARATION:

1. Using a permanent marker, number the underside of each duck, starting with zero.
2. Fill the container half full of water.
3. Float the ducks in the water.

PROCEDURES:

1. The child will wash his or her hands before beginning the activity.
2. The child will select one duck floating in the water.
3. The child will turn the duck over and identify the number written on it. If the child identifies the number correctly, the duck may stay out of the water. If the child is unable to identify the number, the duck is placed back in the water.
4. Continue steps 2–3 until all ducks are out of the water.

AGES: 3–5

DEVELOPMENTAL GOALS:

- ✄ To match colors
- ✄ To enhance number concepts

LEARNING OBJECTIVE:

Using numbered plastic eggs, the child will match colors and numbers.

MATERIALS:

Colored plastic eggs (12)
Permanent marker

Eggs

ADULT PREPARATION:

1. Using a permanent marker, write the number 1 on each half of the first plastic egg. Write the number 2 on each half of the second egg and so on, through egg 12.
2. Take the eggs apart and lay halves on the table in random order.

PROCEDURES:

The child will complete the following steps:

1. Select an egg half and identify its number and color.
2. Find the other egg half bearing the same number.
3. Snap the two halves together.
4. Repeat steps 1–3 until all egg halves are correctly matched.

VARIATION:

Write a number on one half of each egg and draw dots corresponding to that number on the other half of the egg (one dot with the number 1, two dots with the number 2, etc.).

Egg Cartons

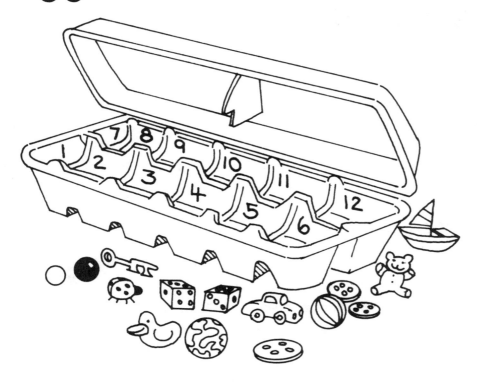

AGES: 3–5

DEVELOPMENTAL GOALS:

✂ To improve counting skills

✂ To recognize numbers

LEARNING OBJECTIVE:

Using egg cartons and counters, the child will identify numbers and count objects.

MATERIALS:

Foam or cardboard egg cartons
Permanent marker
Counters (e.g., buttons, dinosaurs, bears)

ADULT PREPARATION:

1. Using permanent marker, label each section of the egg carton with a numeral (1–12).

2. Place the counters on the table.

PROCEDURES:

The child will complete the following steps:

1. Identify the number on one egg carton section.

2. Count that many counters and place them in that egg carton section.

VARIATION:

Have the child sort various objects into the egg carton sections (e.g., all red items in one section, all blue items in another, etc.).

⚠ SAFETY PRECAUTION:

Maintain close supervision when young children are using small objects, to prevent choking incidents.

Elephants and Peanuts

AGES: 2½–5

DEVELOPMENTAL GOALS:

- ✂ To improve number recognition
- ✂ To acquire rational counting skills

LEARNING OBJECTIVE:

Using bowls, peanuts, and numbered paper elephants, the child will identify numbers and count objects.

MATERIALS:

Elephant pattern
  (Appendix A14)
Permanent marker
Gray construction
  paper
Bowl
Peanuts in the shell

ADULT PREPARATION:

1. Using the elephant pattern, cut 11 elephants out of gray construction paper.
2. Number the elephants 0–10.
3. Place the elephants on the table or floor with a bowl of peanuts.

PROCEDURES:

The child will complete the following steps:

1. Identify the number on an elephant.
2. Count out that many peanuts and "feed" the elephant.
3. Repeat steps 1–2 until all the elephants are fed.

⚠ SAFETY PRECAUTIONS:

If any children in the group have peanut allergies, use packing peanuts instead. Observe young children closely, peanuts may present a choking hazard in very young children.

Eraser Sorting

ADULT PREPARATION:

1. Set an assortment of erasers on the table. Make sure there are multiple amounts of each identical eraser.
2. Put one eraser into each muffin cup (a different type in each cup).

PROCEDURES:

The child will complete the following steps:
1. Identify the kinds of erasers on the table.
2. Select one eraser in a muffin cup.
3. Find all identical erasers and put them together in the muffin cup.
4. Repeat steps 2–3 until all erasers are sorted into sets in the muffin pan.

EXPANSION:

Have the child count the number of erasers in each set.

SAFETY PRECAUTION:

If the erasers are small, observe the children closely to prevent choking incidents.

AGES: 3–5

DEVELOPMENTAL GOALS:

✁ To recognize sets
✁ To improve sorting skills

LEARNING OBJECTIVE:

Using a muffin tin and an assortment of erasers, the child will sort by color, size, and/or shape.

MATERIALS:

Assorted erasers
Muffin tin

F

AGES: 4–5

AGES: 2–3
(match colors
only)

DEVELOPMENTAL GOALS:

- ✂ To identify colors
- ✂ To recognize sets
- ✂ To improve patterning abilities

LEARNING OBJECTIVE:

Using feathers and construction paper, the child will match colors and numbers.

MATERIALS:

Package of assorted feathers

Construction paper in colors to match feathers

Feather Sets

ADULT PREPARATION:

1. Cut 8" × 8" squares of construction paper. Cut one square to match each color of feathers.
2. Lay the squares on the table.
3. Lay feathers on the table in random order.

PROCEDURES:

1. Child will identify the colors of the feathers and squares.
2. Child will match colors by placing all feathers of like color on the same color square.
3. Start an ABC pattern by laying down feathers of three colors in a repeating pattern.
4. Invite child to continue the pattern by laying down a feather of the first color needed to repeat the pattern.
5. Child will continue adding feathers in the ABC pattern.

Note: Children need to be comfortable with creating an AB pattern before the more difficult ABC pattern is attempted.

VARIATION:

Write numbers on paper plates. Have the child identify numbers, count, out feathers, and place that many feathers on each plate.

Fence Weaving

AGES: 3½–5

DEVELOPMENTAL GOALS:

✂ To enhance spatial relationships

✂ To improve patterning skills

LEARNING OBJECTIVE:

Using a chain-link fence, ribbon, and crepe paper streamers, the child will weave a pattern in the fence.

MATERIALS:

Ribbons in assorted lengths, colors, and textures
Crepe paper streamers
Scissors

ADULT PREPARATION:

1. Cut ribbons and crepe paper streamers into various lengths.
2. Tie ribbons and crepe paper streamers to the fence.

PROCEDURES:

1. Discuss with the child how the ribbons and streamers will go in and out of the chain-link fence sections.
2. Child will then weave ribbons and streamers in and out of the fence sections, creating an AB pattern by alternating colors of ribbons and streamers.

⚠ SAFETY PRECAUTION:

Once ribbons and streamers are tied to the fence, the length must not exceed 12 inches. This is to prevent choking hazards.

Fingerprints

DEVELOPMENTAL GOALS:

✄ To recognize numbers

✄ To improve rational counting skills

LEARNING OBJECTIVE:

Using a stamp pad, stapler, and paper squares, the child will create a counting booklet.

MATERIALS:

Washable ink stamp pad
Paper
Scissors
Ruler
Marker
Stapler

ADULT PREPARATION:

1. Using a ruler and scissors, cut paper into 4.5" by 6" rectangles.
2. With the marker, write a separate number on each rectangle.

PROCEDURES:

The child will complete the following steps:

1. Choose a rectangle and identify the number on it.
2. Count and make fingerprints on the rectangle equal to the number, using a washable ink stamp pad.
3. Repeat steps 1–2 until all rectangles (with the exception of the one marked zero) have fingerprints.
4. Arrange the rectangles in numerical order from 0–10.
5. Watch as the rectangles are stapled into a booklet.

Note: Make a set of numbered rectangles (0–10) for each child. Depending on the children's attention span, this project may need to be spread over several days. Knowing the ability of the children may encourage you to use less or more numbers.

VARIATION:

Fingerprints may be turned into bugs, bears, etc. before rectangles are stapled into booklet.

Fishing

ADULT PREPARATION:

1. Using fish pattern, trace fish and then cut out of construction paper.
2. Write numbers 0–10 on the fish with the marker.
3. Attach one paper clip to each fish.
4. If the fishing pole doesn't have a line, attach heavy string to the pole.
5. Tie a magnet to the end of the string.
6. Place construction paper fish in a bucket or container.

PROCEDURES:

The child will complete the following steps:

1. Sit or stand by the bucket of fish.
2. Drop the fishing line, with the magnet attached, into the bucket.
3. Lift the string out of the bucket to see if he or she caught a fish.
4. Identify the number on the fish that was caught.
5. Take the fish off the magnet and place it to one side.
6. Repeat steps 2–5 until all fish are caught.

VARIATIONS:

Instead of writing numbers on the fish, cut out fish in different sizes. Then, as the fish are caught, have the child arrange them in order by size. Or put geometric shapes on the fish and ask the child to identify each shape and sort the fish by shape.

AGES: 3–5

DEVELOPMENTAL GOALS:

- ✂ To recognize numbers
- ✂ To enhance large muscle development

LEARNING OBJECTIVE:

Using a fishing pole, heavy string, magnet, bucket, paper fish, and paper clips, the child will identify numbers.

MATERIALS:

Child-size fishing pole with fishing line or heavy string
Magnet
Construction paper
Fish pattern (Appendix A15)
Scissors
Marker
Paper clips (metal)
Bucket or large container

French Fries

DEVELOPMENTAL GOALS:

- ✄ To recognize numbers
- ✄ To improve rational counting skills
- ✄ To sequence numbers
- ✄ To become familiar with left-to-right progression

LEARNING OBJECTIVE:

Using numbered french fry containers and sponge strips, the child will practice counting and will recognize and sequence numbers in a left-to-right progression.

MATERIALS:

Cardboard french fry containers from fast food restaurants
Construction paper
Rubber cement
Marker
Yellow sponges
Scissors
Bowl

ADULT PREPARATION:

1. Visit fast food restaurants and ask for donations of cardboard french fry containers.
2. Cut construction paper into small squares.
3. Write the numbers 0–10 on the squares.
4. Glue one square on each french fry container.
5. Cut yellow sponges into long strips that resemble french fries.
6. Set french fry containers on the table in random order.
7. Place sponge "french fries" in a bowl and place the bowl on the table.

PROCEDURES:

The child will complete the following steps:

1. Identify the numbers on the french fry containers.
2. Arrange the containers in order from 0–10 and moving from left to right.
3. Select one container and identify the number on it.
4. Count that many french fries and place them in the container.

36

Gingerbread Men

ADULT PREPARATION:

1. Trace pattern and cut gingerbread men from light brown construction paper.
2. Decorate gingerbread men with puff paint.
3. With puff paint, draw a geometric shape in the center of each gingerbread man.
4. When dry, hot-glue magnetic strips to the backs of the gingerbread men.
5. Using a permanent marker, trace the gingerbread pattern onto the cookie sheet. Repeat the pattern until the metal sheet is full. In the center of each gingerbread man, draw a duplicate of a geometric shape that is on one paper gingerbread man.
6. Place cookie sheet on the table.
7. Lay gingerbread men on the table in random order.

PROCEDURES:

The child will complete the following steps:

1. Identify the shapes on the paper gingerbread men.
2. Match the paper gingerbread men to the silhouettes on the tray bearing the same geometric shapes. (Gingerbread men will magnetically adhere to the tray.)

AGES: 2–5

DEVELOPMENTAL GOALS:

✄ To recognize shapes
✄ To acquire classification skills through matching

LEARNING OBJECTIVE:

Using magnetic, construction paper "gingerbread" men and a metal cookie sheet, the child will match shapes.

MATERIALS:

Permanent marker
Metal cookie sheet
Magnetic strips
Hot glue gun and glue sticks
Gingerbread man pattern (Appendix A16)
Light brown construction paper
Scissors
Puff paint (or a couple drops of liquid watercolor mixed with white school glue)

Giraffes and Spots

DEVELOPMENTAL GOALS:

- ✂ To improve number recognition
- ✂ To enhance rational counting skills

LEARNING OBJECTIVE:

Using a giraffe folder game, the child will identify numbers and use rational counting.

MATERIALS:

Giraffe pattern (Appendix A17)
Yellow construction paper
Rubber cement
Scissors
Marker
File folder

ADULT PREPARATION:

1. Trace pattern on yellow construction paper and cut out giraffes.
2. Write numbers, 0–10, on half of the giraffes.
3. Using rubber cement, glue the numbered giraffes on the inside of the folder.
4. Draw spots on the remaining giraffes. Leave one giraffe spotless. Draw one spot on one giraffe, two spots on another, etc., until all numbered giraffes on the folder have corresponding spotted giraffes.
5. Place folder on the table.
6. Lay spotted giraffes on the table in random order.

PROCEDURES:

The child will complete the following steps:

1. Identify the numbers on the giraffes on the folder.
2. Select a giraffe with spots and count the spots.
3. Place spotted giraffe on top of the corresponding numbered giraffe.
4. Repeat steps 1–3 until all giraffes are matched.

VARIATION:

Cut 4½" by 6" rectangles. Glue spotless giraffes on the rectangles. Write numbers, starting with zero, on each rectangle. Give each child a set of these giraffe cards. The child will identify the number and then glue or stamp that many spots on the giraffe. When dry, the cards may be stapled into a counting giraffe booklet for each child.

Goats and Trash

ADULT PREPARATION:

1. Trace pattern and cut goat heads out of construction paper.
2. Open paper bags.
3. Staple one goat head to the front of each bag.
4. Cut out the goat's mouth, cutting an opening into the paper bag.
5. Number each bag, 0–10.
6. Stand bags on the table in random order.
7. Set "trash" on a plate.

PROCEDURES:

The child will complete the following steps:

1. Identify numbers on the goat head bags.
2. Sequence bags from left to right in numerical order, starting with zero.
3. Select a bag and identify its number.
4. Count out pieces of trash to match the bag's number and "feed" it into the goat's mouth.
5. Repeat step 3 until all of the goats have been fed their corresponding number of trash pieces.

AGES: 3–5

DEVELOPMENTAL GOALS:

- ✂ To improve number recognition
- ✂ To enhance rational counting skills
- ✂ To sequence numbers
- ✂ To use left-to-right progression

LEARNING OBJECTIVE:

Using "trash" and numbered goat head bags, the child will practice counting and will recognize and sequence numbers in a left-to-right progression.

MATERIALS:

Lunch-size paper bags
Goat head pattern (Appendix A18)
Construction paper
Scissors
Stapler
Marker
Trash (bottle caps, scraps of paper, foil, etc.)
Foam plate

Golf Tees

DEVELOPMENTAL GOALS:

✄ To recognize numbers

✄ To enhance rational counting skills

✄ To recognize one-to-one correspondence

✄ To improve fine motor skills

LEARNING OBJECTIVE:

Using wooden blocks with holes drilled in them and golf tees, the child will recognize numbers and practice counting and one-to-one correspondence.

MATERIALS:

Wooden blocks
Goggles
Sandpaper
C-clamp
Broad-tipped perma-
    nent marker
Small hand drill
Golf tees
Bowl
Optional: nontoxic
    paint and brush

ADULT PREPARATION:

1. Have blocks cut into 4" by 4" squares. (Do not use lumber that is treated for outdoor use.)

2. Wearing goggles, sand the blocks smooth. (Optional: Paint the block and let it dry overnight.)

3. Write a number on each block from 0–10 with broad-tipped marker.

4. Use a C-clamp to secure a block to the table.

5. Wearing goggles, drill as many holes in the block as its number indicates.

6. Brush any sawdust away and sand again if necessary.

7. Set the blocks on the table.

8. Pour golf tees into a bowl and set them on the table.

continued

Golf Tees continued

PROCEDURES:

The child will complete the following steps:

1. Identify the number on a block.
2. Count out golf tees to match that number.
3. Place a golf tee in each hole, filling the block's holes with counted golf tees.
4. Repeat steps 1 to 4 until all blocks contain golf tees.

Note: This activity is self-checking, because the child will recognize when he or she has counted too many or too few golf tees for a block's holes.

VARIATIONS:

Blocks may be cut out in the shapes of numbers. STYROFOAM may be used in place of wooden blocks.

⚠ SAFETY PRECAUTION:

Supervise younger children closely when they are handling golf tees. Also, children may help with preparation, using child-size hand tools, but they should not be allowed to use power tools.

Groundhogs and Shadows

AGES: 3–5

DEVELOPMENTAL GOALS:

- ✄ To enhance classification skills through matching
- ✄ To recognize one-to-one correspondence

LEARNING OBJECTIVE:

Using paper groundhogs and shadows, the child will match items by size and one-to-one correspondence.

MATERIALS:

Groundhog patterns (Appendix A19)
Brown and black construction paper
Scissors
Marker

ADULT PREPARATION:

1. Trace pattern and cut out groundhogs in assorted sizes, using brown paper.
2. Using a marker, add facial features to the brown groundhogs.
3. Cut an identical assortment of groundhogs out of black paper. (These are the groundhog shadows.)
4. Lay the groundhogs on the table.
5. Place the shadows on the table in a stack.

PROCEDURES:

The child will complete the following steps:

1. Select a shadow from the stack and find its matching groundhog.
2. Repeat step 1 until all of the groundhogs have found their shadows.

EXPANSION:

Sequence the groundhogs by size, from smallest to largest.

Hair Colors

AGES: 3–5

DEVELOPMENTAL GOALS:

- ✂ To understand graphing
- ✂ To acquire rational counting skills
- ✂ To improve classification skills

LEARNING OBJECTIVE:

Using pictures of children, a glue stick, and a poster chart, the children will create a graph.

MATERIALS:

Poster board
Markers
Yardstick
Pictures of children
Glue stick

ADULT PREPARATION:

1. Using markers and a yardstick, draw a chart on a poster board.
2. Write the chart title "Hair Color" at the top of the poster.
3. Divide the chart into columns equaling the total number of different hair colors in the classroom (e.g., blond, brown, black, red).
4. Label the bottom of each column with a hair color, writing with a marker that matches that hair color (e.g., yellow marker for blond).
5. Cut out a small picture of each child.

PROCEDURES:

1. Give each child the picture of himself or herself.
2. Read the hair color choices at the bottom of the chart.
3. Ask, "Who has black hair?"

continued

Hair Colors continued

4. The children with black hair will glue their pictures in the black column of the chart, in a vertical line. The first picture should be placed at the bottom.

5. Repeat steps 3–4 with children having blond, brown, and red hair.

6. When all the pictures are glued on the chart, count the number of children in each column.

7. Ask the children, "Which hair color has the greatest number?" and "Which hair color has the least number?"

Hats

AGES: 2½–5

DEVELOPMENTAL GOALS:

- ✄ To promote classification through matching
- ✄ To recognize colors
- ✄ To identify sets

LEARNING OBJECTIVE:

Using hats, the child will match colors and create sets.

MATERIALS:

Variety of hats
Laundry basket

ADULT PREPARATION:

1. Ask families to send in an assortment of hats (e.g., baby hats, ball caps, winter hats, cowboy hats).
2. Ask families to label their hats with masking tape, if they would like them returned.
3. If families are unable to lend any hats, purchase hats at thrift stores.
4. Place hats in laundry basket.

PROCEDURES:

The child will complete the following steps:

1. Take hats out of laundry basket and lay them on the table.
2. Sort the hats by type (baby, sports, winter, cowboy, etc.).

continued

Hats continued

3. Count the number in each set.
4. Identify the hat colors and sort them by color.

VARIATION:

As a large group activity, have each child select a hat to wear. Ask the children to sort themselves by their hat colors (e.g., "If you're wearing a red hat, stand beside the cubbies"). Make certain that hats are washable if children wear them.

Homes

ADULT PREPARATION:

1. Pick up several real estate booklets.
2. Cut out duplicate pictures of 5–10 homes.
3. Glue one set of pictures to the inside of a folder.
4. Glue the other set to squares of construction paper.
5. Staple the resealable plastic bag to the back of the folder (see "Helpful Hints," page xi), providing a place to store the home cards.
6. Lay folder and home cards on the table.

PROCEDURES:

The child will complete the following steps:
1. Select a home card.
2. Note color, and placement of windows and doors.
3. Find the identical home on the folder.
4. Lay the home card on the matching home on the folder.
5. Repeat steps 1–4 until all homes are matched.

AGES: 2–5

DEVELOPMENTAL GOALS:

✀ To use classification by matching
✀ To make comparisons

LEARNING OBJECTIVE:

Using a folder game, the children will match similar pictures of homes.

MATERIALS:

Real estate booklets that show homes for sale
File folder
Rubber cement
Construction paper
Scissors
Resealable plastic bag
Stapler

47

Horses

AGES: 3–5

AGE: 2 (match shapes on baskets and horses)

DEVELOPMENTAL GOALS:

- ✂ To recognize numbers
- ✂ To practice rational counting
- ✂ To demonstrate classification skills
- ✂ To understand spatial concepts

LEARNING OBJECTIVE:

Using berry baskets and plastic horses, the child will recognize numbers, practice counting, sort objects, and use spatial concepts.

MATERIALS:

Several sets of plastic horses
Berry baskets (to use as corrals)
Paper
Scissors
Marker
Tape

ADULT PREPARATION:

1. Cut paper into 2" squares.
2. Write a number on each square, starting with zero through 10.
3. Tape numbers to the berry baskets.
4. Place baskets on the table in random order.
5. Place plastic horses on the table.

PROCEDURES:

1. Child will identify numbers on a berry basket "corral" and count out that number of horses to place in the corral.
2. To have the child practice sorting, turn the basket around so that its number is not visible to him or her, then ask child to sort horses into the basket by color or size.
3. Practice recognition of spatial relationships by asking the child to put the horse in, beside, or in front of the corral (or use two corrals and ask that the horse be put between them).

Note: If plastic horses are not available, cut out horses that will fit inside the berry baskets.

Hot Air Balloons

ADULT PREPARATION:

1. Trace patterns and cut out hot air balloons and baskets (two balloons and two baskets of each color).
2. Cut small shapes out of various colors of paper. Cut two of each color.
3. Glue matching shapes on matching baskets and balloons (e.g., glue a blue triangle on one yellow balloon and one yellow basket; glue a purple circle on the second yellow balloon and basket).

PROCEDURES:

1. Lay baskets and balloons on the table in random order.
2. Show child a balloon.
3. Ask the child to identify the color of the balloon.
4. Ask the child to identify the shape on the balloon.
5. Child then can find the identical color of basket and shape.
6. Repeat steps 2–5 until all balloons and baskets are matched.

AGES: 2–5

DEVELOPMENTAL GOALS:

- ✂ To identify colors
- ✂ To recognize shapes

LEARNING OBJECTIVE:

Using paper hot air balloons and baskets, the child will match and recognize colors and shapes.

MATERIALS:

Hot air balloon and basket patterns (Appendix A20)
Paper in various colors
Pencil
Scissors
Rubber cement

Ice

DEVELOPMENTAL GOALS:

- ✂ To practice measurement
- ✂ To identify weight
- ✂ To develop number concepts
- ✂ To enhance fine motor skills

LEARNING OBJECTIVE:

Using tongs, a balance scale, and ice cubes, the child will learn the concept of heavier and lighter weights and will practice counting.

MATERIALS:

Tongs
Balance scale with buckets
Ice
Bowl
Large towel

ADULT PREPARATION:

1. Place ice cubes in a bowl.
2. Cover the table with a large towel.
3. Set the bowl of ice cubes, tongs, and balance scale on the table.

PROCEDURES:

1. Child will use tongs to pick up ice cubes and transfer them to the balance scale buckets.
2. Ask the child to put one cube in the first bucket and five cubes in the second bucket.
3. Ask the child to describe the difference in the scale's buckets.
4. Inform the child that the bucket that is lower is heavier, and the bucket that is higher is lighter.

continued

Ice continued

5. Ask the child, "What makes the lower bucket heavier than the other one?"

6. Listen to the child's response. If the child's answer is incorrect, lead him or her to the conclusion that the bucket with more ice cubes is heavier and the bucket with less ice cubes is lighter.

7. Vary the number of ice cubes in each bucket and ask the child to count them.

8. Again ask the child to identify either the heavier or lighter side.

Ice Cream

AGES: 3–5

AGE: 2 (match shapes or colors)

DEVELOPMENTAL GOALS:

- ✂ To recognize numbers
- ✂ To use rational counting

LEARNING OBJECTIVE:

Using cutouts of ice cream scoops and cones, the child will practice counting and recognize numbers.

MATERIALS:

Brown, pink, white, and yellow construction paper
Ice cream cone pattern (Appendix A21)
Scissors
Marker
Laminator and laminating film, or clear contact paper

ADULT PREPARATION:

1. Trace pattern and cut out 11 yellow cones.
2. Using a marker, number the cones 0–10.
3. Trace pattern and cut out 55 scoops of ice cream, using pink, white, and brown construction paper.
4. Laminate all pieces or cover with clear contact paper for durability.
5. Put the ice cream scoops in a bowl or a clean ice cream container and place it on the table.
6. Place the cones on the table in random order.

PROCEDURES:

The child will complete the following steps:

1. Select a cone and identify the number on the cone.
2. Count and place that many scoops of ice cream on the cone.
3. Continue steps 1–2 until all cones (except the one numbered zero) have scoops of ice cream.

52

Igloo

ADULT PREPARATION:

1. Enlarge the pattern of an igloo to fill the poster board.
2. Trace pattern and cut the igloo from each poster board.
3. Draw large interlocking puzzle pieces on one igloo, then cut the igloo pieces apart.
4. Trace each of the puzzle pieces from the first igloo onto the remaining igloo, then outline them with marker. (Do not cut these out.)
5. Cut and glue geometric shapes on each puzzle piece, also gluing a matching shape on the corresponding section of the complete igloo.
6. Set complete igloo and matching puzzle pieces on the table.

PROCEDURES:

The child will complete the following steps:

1. Select a puzzle piece and identify the shape glued on it.
2. Find the section of the complete igloo that contains the same shape and put the puzzle piece on it.
3. Repeat steps 1–2 until the igloo puzzle is finished.

AGES: 3–5

AGE: 2 (use fewer and larger pieces)

DEVELOPMENTAL GOALS:

- ✂ To recognize basic shapes
- ✂ To increase fine motor skills

LEARNING OBJECTIVE:

Using an igloo puzzle, the child will recognize shapes.

MATERIALS:

Two pieces of poster board or tag board
Igloo pattern (Appendix A22)
Scissors
Construction paper
Yardstick
Marker
Rubber cement

Jacks and Balls

AGE: 5

DEVELOPMENTAL GOALS:

- ✂ To use rational counting
- ✂ To recognize numbers
- ✂ To improve eye-hand coordination

LEARNING OBJECTIVE:

Using jacks, a ball, and number cards, the child will recognize numbers and practice counting.

MATERIALS:

Large jacks and ball
Construction paper
Marker
Scissors
Cup

ADULT PREPARATION:

1. Cut construction paper into squares approximately 3" x 5".
2. Number the squares 0–10.
3. Lay the squares face down on the table.
4. Set the jacks, ball, and a cup on the table.

PROCEDURES:

The child will complete the following steps:

1. Turn over a numbered square.
2. Identify the number and pick up that many jacks, putting them into a cup.
3. Bounce the ball as many times as the number on the square, counting out loud as it bounces.
4. Pick up cup and empty the jacks back onto the table.
5. Repeat steps 1–4 until all cards are flipped over.

54

Jelly Beans

ADULT PREPARATION:

1. Buy individual packs of jelly beans, or divide jelly beans into individual resealable plastic bags.
2. Make a copy of the graph (Appendix A23) for each child.
3. Using crayons or colored pencils, fill in the bottom row of each graph with one of each jelly bean color to be used.
4. Set small plates on the table.
5. Place one jelly bean of each color on its own plate.
6. Set glue, graphs, and jelly beans on the table.
7. Give each child an individual bag of jelly beans, some glue, and a graph.

PROCEDURES:

The child will complete the following steps:

1. Identify the color of the jelly bean on each plate.
2. Sort jelly beans onto the plates according to color.
3. Identify the color of the jelly bean at the bottom of the first column.
4. Glue all jelly beans matching that color in the first column.
5. Repeat steps 3–4 with the other columns, until all jelly beans have been glued on the graph.
6. Count the number of jelly beans in each column.
7. Count jelly beans and respond correctly when asked, "Which color has the most jelly beans?"
8. Count jelly beans and respond correctly when asked, "Which color has the least jelly beans?"

Note: Four- and five-year-olds are able to count the jelly beans and then color each square representing a jelly bean. Younger children do not have this ability and need to place actual objects on the squares.

SAFETY PRECAUTION:

Supervise young children closely as jelly beans may be a choking hazard.

AGES: 3–5

DEVELOPMENTAL GOALS:

- ✂ To identify colors
- ✂ To enhance classification through sorting
- ✂ To use rational counting
- ✂ To develop graphing skills

LEARNING OBJECTIVE:

Using jelly beans, small plates, a graph, and glue, the child will create a graph by identifying, sorting, and counting colors.

MATERIALS:

Jelly beans
Graph (Appendix A23)
Crayons or colored pencils
Resealable plastic bags
Small plates
White school glue

Jewels

AGES: 3–5

DEVELOPMENTAL GOALS:

- ✂ To recognize shapes
- ✂ To identify colors
- ✂ To use classification by matching
- ✂ To increase fine motor skills

LEARNING OBJECTIVE:

Using a small poster board and simulated jewels, the child will identify colors and recognize and match shapes.

MATERIALS:

Decorative simulated jewels (flat on one side)
Quarter sheet of poster board or tag board
Markers
Bowl

ADULT PREPARATION:

1. Trace different jewels onto small sheet of poster board.
2. Color the tracing with markers to match the jewel colors.
3. Place the jewels in a bowl.
4. Place the bowl and poster board on the table.

PROCEDURES:

The child will complete the following steps:

1. Choose a jewel from the bowl.
2. Identify the color and shape of the jewel.
3. Find the silhouette matching that jewel on the poster board.
4. Place the jewel on its poster board match.
5. Repeat steps 1–4 until all jewels are matched with the poster board.

⚠ SAFETY PRECAUTION:

Supervise young children closely, because small jewels may be a choking hazard.

Kangaroos

ADULT PREPARATION:

1. Trace patterns and cut out 11 kangaroos and 11 joeys.
2. Write a number (0–10) on each kangaroo's pocket.
3. Draw dots (0–10) on each joey.
4. Using the box cutter, make a slit in the top of the kangaroo's pocket that is large enough for the joey.
5. Set the kangaroos on the table in random order.
6. Set the joeys on the table in a stack.

PROCEDURES:

The child will complete the following steps:
1. Pick a joey from the stack.
2. Count the number of dots on the joey.
3. Find the same number on a kangaroo's pocket.
4. Fit the joey into the slit in the kangaroo's pocket.
5. Repeat steps 1–4 until all joeys are in the correct kangaroos' pockets.

AGES: 3–5

DEVELOPMENTAL GOALS:

✷ To recognize numbers

✷ To use rational counting

✷ To enhance eye-hand coordination

LEARNING OBJECTIVE:

Using paper kangaroos and joeys, the child will recognize numbers and count dots.

MATERIALS:

Kangaroo and joey patterns (Appendix A24)
Paper
Marker
Scissors
Box cutter

K

AGES: 4–5

AGES: 2–3 (use less cars and large, unique keys)

DEVELOPMENTAL GOALS:

- ✂ To discriminate between similarities and differences
- ✂ To classify objects by matching them
- ✂ To increase fine motor coordination

LEARNING OBJECTIVE:

Using keys and paper cars, the child will match key shapes.

MATERIALS:

Keys
Car pattern
   (Appendix A25)
Paper
Scissors
Fine-tipped marker

Keys

ADULT PREPARATION:

1. Invite parents or family members to donate discarded keys.
2. Trace pattern and cut out cars.
3. Using a fine-tipped marker, trace the shape of each key onto a car.
4. Set the cars and keys on the table.

PROCEDURES:

The child will complete the following steps:

1. Select a key.
2. Find the car with the matching key pattern drawn on it and lay the key on that car.
3. Repeat steps 1–2 until all keys are matched with the correct cars.

Kites

ADULT PREPARATION:

1. Trace pattern and cut out 22 kites (two of each color).
2. Punch a hole in the bottom of each kite.
3. Thread a 6" length of string through the hole and tie it, making a tail for the kite.
4. On one side of each kite, write a number (0–10). Write the same number on each color-matched pair of kites (e.g., both purple kites have the number 9).
5. On the other side of each kite, draw a shape. Make sure the shapes are identical on kites of the same color (e.g., both purple kites have the oval shape). The same shape can be used on more than one color, however (i.e., both red kites and purple kites may display the oval shape).
6. Lay the kites on the table.

PROCEDURES:

1. Ask the child to identify the colors of the kites on the table.
2. Ask the child to match the kites by putting those of the same color together.
3. When all the kites are matched by color, ask the child to separate the kites by shape.
4. When all the kites are separated into groups by shape, help the child mix them randomly on the table.
5. Ask the child to flip all the kites over so that the number sides are facing up.
6. Ask the child to identify and match the numbers of the kites.
7. When all the kites are matched by number, ask the child to separate the matching pairs and flip all the kites over so that the shape sides are facing up.
8. Ask the child to identify the shapes drawn on the kites.
9. Ask the child to match the kites by shape.

Note: Younger children do not have a sufficient attention span to match the kites three different ways, so choose one or two forms of matching for them.

AGES: 2–5

DEVELOPMENTAL GOALS:

- ✄ To recognize shapes
- ✄ To identify colors
- ✄ To identify numbers
- ✄ To increase classification skills through matching

LEARNING OBJECTIVE:

Using a miniature paper kite, the child will recognize and match shapes, colors, and numbers.

MATERIALS:

Kite pattern (Appendix A26)
Paper in 11 different colors
Scissors
Marker
Hole puncher
String for tail

Koala

AGES: 3–5

DEVELOPMENTAL GOALS:

- ✄ To develop an understanding of spatial relationships
- ✄ To follow directions

LEARNING OBJECTIVE:

Using a paper tree and koala, the child will follow spatial directions in placing the objects.

MATERIALS:

Tree and koala patterns (Appendix A27)
Paper
Scissors
Marker
Large resealable plastic bag (for storage)

ADULT PREPARATION:

1. Trace koala pattern and cut out one koala for each child.
2. Trace tree pattern and cut out two trees for each child.

PROCEDURES:

1. Give each child a koala bear and a tree.
2. Ask the child to put the koala **in** the tree.
3. Ask the child to put the koala **beside** the tree.
4. Ask the child to put the koala **on top of** the tree.
5. Ask the child to put the koala **under** the tree.
6. Give each child a second tree.
7. Ask the child to put the koala **between** the trees.
8. Ask the children to put the koalas and the trees **in** the plastic bag.

60

Ladybugs

ADULT PREPARATION:

1. Trace patterns, then color and cut out at least five ladybugs of graduated sizes.
2. Trace patterns, then color and cut out at least five leaves of graduated sizes.
3. Place leaves and ladybugs on the table.

PROCEDURES:

The child will complete the following steps:

1. Find the smallest ladybug.
2. Lay the ladybug on the far left.
3. Find the next largest ladybug and set it to the right of the first ladybug.
4. Continue until all ladybugs are lined up by size, smallest to largest.
5. Repeat steps 1–4 with leaves, lining them up from smallest to largest from left to right, either above or underneath the row of ladybugs.
6. Match each leaf to the same size ladybug (e.g., the smallest leaf goes to the smallest ladybug).

VARIATION:

Write numbers on the ladybugs and have the child feed the ladybug as many leaves as the number on its back.

AGES: 3–5

DEVELOPMENTAL GOALS:

- ✂ To sequence by size
- ✂ To recognize one-to-one correspondence

LEARNING OBJECTIVE:

Using paper leaves and ladybugs, the child will sequence and match objects by size.

MATERIALS:

Ladybug and leaf patterns (Appendix A28)
Paper
Markers
Scissors

61

Leaf Sorting

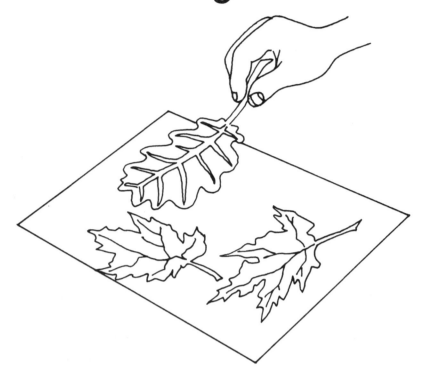

AGES: 3–5

AGE: 2 (sort the leaves by color)

DEVELOPMENTAL GOALS:

- ✄ To enhance classification skills
- ✄ To promote social development by taking turns

LEARNING OBJECTIVE:

Using leaves, a basket, and construction paper, the child will sort and match objects.

MATERIALS:

Leaves
Basket
Construction paper

ADULT PREPARATION:

1. Ask children to bring in a variety of leaves.
2. Place leaves in a basket.
3. Lay pieces of construction paper on the floor in a line.

PROCEDURES:

1. Ask children to sit in a row at least three feet in front of the line of construction paper.
2. Ask the first child to select a leaf from the basket and put it on the first piece of construction paper.
3. Ask the second child to select a leaf from the basket. Tell the child, "If the leaf is different from _____'s leaf, you may put it on the next piece of paper. If the leaf is the same as _____'s leaf, you may put it with _____'s leaf."

continued

62

Leaf Sorting continued

4. Continue, with all children taking turns sorting leaves.

5. When all leaves are sorted, ask the children to count the number of each kind of leaf. Write the number on the construction paper under each set of leaves.

6. Ask the children to arrange the leaves and construction paper from the smallest number to the largest number.

VARIATION:

Cut leaves from construction paper, varying the colors.

Leprechaun's Gold

AGES: 3–5

AGE: 2
(numbers 0–5)

DEVELOPMENTAL GOALS:

- ✄ To develop number concepts
- ✄ To improve eye-hand coordination

LEARNING OBJECTIVE:

Using black pots and "gold nuggets," the child will recognize numbers and use rational counting.

MATERIALS:

Black plastic cups, or black construction paper and leprechaun's pot pattern (Appendix A29)
Rocks
Gold spray paint
White sticky labels or masking tape
Marker

ADULT PREPARATION:

1. Spray paint rocks gold.
2. Write numbers (0–10) on white sticky labels or masking tape.
3. Stick the numbers on 11 black cups.
4. To make the activity self-correcting, put the corresponding number of dots on the bottom of the cups (or on the back of the paper leprechaun pots).
5. Set the leprechaun's pots and the gold rocks on the table.

PROCEDURES:

1. Tell the child, "The leprechaun's gold has fallen out of his pots. Would you please help put it back?"
2. Ask the child to identify the number on the first leprechaun's pot.
3. Ask the child to place that many gold rocks in the pot.
4. Continue until all pots have the correct number of gold rocks.

VARIATION:

Hide the gold rocks. Give the child a leprechaun's pot with a number written on it. Ask the child to find as many pieces of gold as that number and put them in the leprechaun's pot.

Magazine Matching

ADULT PREPARATION:

1. Ask families to send in discarded magazines.
2. Find duplicate magazine covers and cut them off the magazines.
3. Laminate the covers.
4. Place magazine covers on the table.

PROCEDURES:

The child will complete the following steps:
1. Select a magazine cover, then find another cover that is the same.
2. Put covers that are alike together.
3. Continue until all covers are matched.

AGES: 2–5

DEVELOPMENTAL GOALS:

✂ To improve classification skills

✂ To promote visual discrimination

LEARNING OBJECTIVE:

Using magazine covers, the child will match objects.

MATERIALS:

Magazines
Scissors
Laminator and laminating film, or clear contact paper

Mailboxes

AGES: 3–5

AGE: 2 (match shapes or colors or numbers up to 5)

DEVELOPMENTAL GOALS:

✂ To recognize numbers

✂ To enhance eye-hand coordination

✂ To understand one-to-one correspondence

LEARNING OBJECTIVE:

Using "mailboxes" and "envelopes," the child will match numbers.

MATERIALS:

Mailbox and
   flag patterns
   (Appendix A30)
Blue construction paper
Red tag board
Scissors
Marker
Envelopes
Large bag with
   shoulder strap
Brads

ADULT PREPARATION:

1. Trace patterns and cut out 11 mailboxes from construction paper and 11 flags from red tag board.
2. Attach a flag to each mailbox with a brad.
3. Write numbers (0–10) on the flags or mailboxes.
4. Write numbers (0–10) on envelopes.
5. Set mailboxes on the table in random order.
6. Place envelopes in the large shoulder-strap bag.

PROCEDURES:

The child will complete the following steps:

1. Put letter bag over one shoulder.
2. Select a letter from the bag and identify the number on the envelope.
3. Deliver the envelope to the mailbox with the same number.
4. Repeat steps 2–3 until all the mail is delivered.

Note: Mailboxes may be made out of shoeboxes. Cut flags from red tag board, write numbers on the flags, and attach them to the boxes with a brad. Cut a slit in the lid of the shoe box with a box cutter, for the child to "deliver" their mail.

Money Matching

ADULT PREPARATION:

1. Collect four cardboard or plastic cans (all the same size and style) with plastic lids.
2. Cover the cans with contact paper.
3. Select a plastic or real penny, nickel, dime, and quarter.
4. Hot-glue each coin to the side of one can, about halfway down its length.
5. Using the box cutter, cut a slit in each plastic lid. The slit should be large enough for a quarter to slide through.
6. Snap a lid on each can.
7. Place an assortment of coins in a bowl.
8. Set the cans and the coins on the table with the coins on the cans facing the child.

continued

AGES: 4–5

DEVELOPMENTAL GOALS:

- To identify coins
- To improve classification skills

LEARNING OBJECTIVE:

Using cans and coins, the child will identify, sort, and match money.

MATERIALS:

Small cardboard or plastic cans with plastic lids (e.g., tennis ball or potato chip cans)
Box cutter
Plastic or real coins
Contact paper
Scissors
Hot glue gun and glue sticks
Bowl

Money Matching continued

PROCEDURES:

The child will complete the following steps:

1. When asked, point to the can with the penny.
2. Find all the pennies in the bowl and put them into the slot in the top of the penny can.
3. Find the can with the nickel.
4. Find all the nickels in the bowl and place them in the nickel can.
5. Find the can with the dime, then find all the dimes in the bowl and place them in the can.
6. Find the can with the quarter, then find all the quarters in the bowl and place them in the can.

Note: When the child is finished, empty the cans to ensure that only the type of coin designated for each can was placed inside it.

⊘ SAFETY PRECAUTION:

When working with young children, maintain close supervision to ensure that they do not put coins into their mouths. Money stickers on small pieces of construction paper may be used as a replacement for coins.

Monkeys

ADULT PREPARATION:

1. Trace patterns, then color and cut out 11 monkeys and 55 bananas.
2. Write a number on each monkey (0–10).
3. Using rubber cement, glue the monkeys inside a file folder.
4. Staple the resealable plastic bag to the back of the folder (see "Helpful Hints," page xi), providing a place to store the banana cutouts.
5. Place the bananas in a bowl.
6. Place the bowl and file folder on the table.

PROCEDURES:

1. Show the child the monkeys in the folder.
2. Ask the child to identify the numbers on the monkeys.
3. Tell the child that these monkeys need to be fed, and they are only to get as many bananas as their number allows.
4. Have the child select a monkey and identify the number written on that monkey.
5. Have the child count out the specified number of bananas and place them on the monkey.
6. Repeat until all monkeys are "fed."

AGES: 3–5

**AGE: 2
(numbers 0–5)**

DEVELOPMENTAL GOALS:

- ✂ To enhance number concepts
- ✂ To improve problem-solving skills

LEARNING OBJECTIVE:

Using a file folder and paper monkeys and bananas, the child will identify numbers and count objects.

MATERIALS:

Monkey and banana patterns (Appendix A31)
File folder
Paper
Markers, colored pencils, or crayons
Scissors
Rubber cement
Bowl
Resealable plastic bag
Stapler

AGES: 2¹/₂–5

DEVELOPMENTAL GOALS:

- ✄ To increase classification skills through matching
- ✄ To enlarge vocabulary

LEARNING OBJECTIVE:

Using pictures of mother animals and baby animals, the child will identify and match animals.

MATERIALS:

Pictures of mother animals and baby animals (or plastic animals)
Scissors
Construction paper
Rubber cement

Mother Animals and Baby Animals

ADULT PREPARATION:

1. Find separate pictures of animals and their offspring in magazines, clip art, or Internet sources.
2. Cut and glue pictures on pieces of construction paper that are all the same size.
3. Lay pictures on the table in random order.

PROCEDURES:

1. Ask child to identify the pictures on the table.
2. Have child select one baby animal and then find its mother.
3. Put the paired animals together and set them aside.
4. Repeat steps 2–3 until all mothers and babies have been matched.

Nails

ADULT PREPARATION:

1. Wearing goggles, sand blocks until smooth.
2. With a marker, draw one number on each block (0–10).
3. Using a hammer, outline the number on each block with nails. The nails should be securely in the block but protruding at least 2 inches above the wood, and they should be approximately 1" apart.
4. Set the nail boards and a container of rubber bands on the table.

PROCEDURES:

1. Show the child the nail boards.
2. Say, "The nails are in the shape of numbers. What are the numbers?"
3. Help the child identify all the numbers on the blocks.
4. Show the child how to wind rubber bands around the nails.

EXPANSION:

Have the child count out rubber bands equal to the number on the nail board and wind only that many around the numeral formed by nails.

VARIATION:

Nails and wood may be replaced with golf tees and STYROFOAM. Pegs and peg boards may also be used. Close supervision is necessary if using golf tees with young children.

AGE: 5

AGES: 3–4 (use the materials listed in the variation)

DEVELOPMENTAL GOALS:

- ✂ To recognize numbers
- ✂ To develop small muscles

LEARNING OBJECTIVE:

Using nail boards and rubber bands, the child will identify numbers.

MATERIALS:

Nails
Six-inch squares of wood
Sandpaper
Goggles
Hammer
Marker
Rubber bands
Container with lid or resealable plastic bags (to store rubber bands)

DEVELOPMENTAL GOALS:

✄ To comprehend patterning

✄ To improve eye-hand coordination

LEARNING OBJECTIVE:

Using yarn, cereal, beads, or foam pieces, the child will create a pattern while stringing a necklace.

MATERIALS:

Yarn
White school glue
Scissors
Wax paper
Objects to string on necklace (different types of cereal, beads, foam shapes, etc.)

Necklace

ADULT PREPARATION:

1. Cut the yarn into lengths long enough to tie into a necklace, but no longer than 12".

2. Dip one end of the yarn in glue and lay on wax paper to dry overnight. (The yarn hardens into a "needle" for the child.)

3. Tie a stopper (e.g., a piece of cereal, a bead) on the other end of the yarn to keep objects from falling off after the child strings them.

4. Place objects to be strung in individual bowls.

5. Set the bowls on the table with the yarn.

PROCEDURES:

1. Allow each child to select two types of items to string on his or her necklace.

2. Ask each child to count out five of each item.

3. Children then string the items on the yarn, alternating objects in an AB pattern.

Notes: Depending on age and attention span, a child may choose to count out more items to add to the pattern. A child with more practice in patterning may advance to an ABC pattern (red, blue, green, red, blue, green) or an ABBA pattern (red, blue, blue, red, red, blue, blue, red). Younger children have more success stringing with a pipe cleaner. Two long pipe cleaners may be twisted together to form a necklace, or use just one to create a bracelet.

Net Full of Numbers

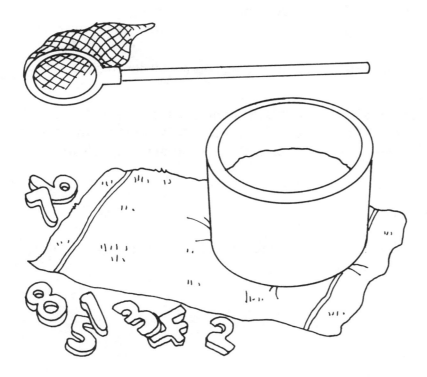

AGES: 2½–5

DEVELOPMENTAL GOALS:

✂ To improve number recognition

✂ To increase muscle development

LEARNING OBJECTIVE:

Using a fish net, plastic numbers, and a tub of water, the child will identify numbers.

MATERIALS:

Small fish net
Plastic numbers
Plastic container
Towel

ADULT PREPARATION:

1. Fill a plastic container half full of water.
2. Lay a large towel on the table.
3. Set the container of water on the towel.
4. Place the plastic numbers in the water.
5. Set the net beside the tub.

PROCEDURES:

The child will complete the following steps:

1. Dip the net into the water, scoop up one number, and lay it on the towel.

continued

Net Full of Numbers continued

2. Identify the number. (A number that is identified correctly may stay on the towel, but a number that is not identified correctly must be placed back in the water.)

3. Continue steps 1–2 until all numbers are identified correctly.

Note: Limit the amount of plastic numbers in the water for young children, to accommodate their shorter attention span. This activity may be done either inside or outside, using the sensory/water table.

VARIATION:

In place of numbers, use plastic geometric shapes to promote shape and/or color recognition.

Nuts

ADULT PREPARATION:

1. Place mixed nuts in a bowl.
2. Set the bowl of nuts and a sectioned tray on the table.
3. Select one of each type of nut and put them in individual compartments of the tray.

PROCEDURE:

The child will complete the following step:

1. Sort through the bowl of nuts, putting nuts that are alike into different sections of the tray.

EXPANSIONS:

Count the number of each kind of nut, sequence the nuts by size, or create an AB pattern with the nuts (e.g., walnut, pecan, walnut, pecan).

⚠ SAFETY PRECAUTION:

Supervise children closely, because nuts may be a choking hazard. Do not use this activity with children who are allergic to nuts.

AGES: 3–5

DEVELOPMENTAL GOALS:

✂ To promote classification through sorting
✂ To match objects that are alike

LEARNING OBJECTIVE:

Using a bowl of mixed nuts and a sectioned tray, the child will sort nuts.

MATERIALS:

Bowl
Bag of mixed nuts in the shell
Sectioned tray (a muffin pan may be used)

Octagons

DEVELOPMENTAL GOALS:

- ✂ To identify the shape of an octagon
- ✂ To sequence objects by size
- ✂ To become familiar with left-to-right progression

LEARNING OBJECTIVE:

Using paper octagons of various sizes, the child will recognize the octagonal shape and sequence objects by size.

MATERIALS:

Octagon pattern (Appendix A32)
Copy paper
Construction paper
Scissors

ADULT PREPARATION:

1. Trace octagon pattern on copy paper.
2. Use a copier to either enlarge or reduce the pattern.
3. Trace the patterns on construction paper and cut out octagons of various sizes.
4. Lay octagons on the table in random order.

PROCEDURES:

1. Show child the shapes on the table.
2. Ask child, "What is the name of this shape?"
3. If the child doesn't respond correctly, say, "It is an octagon. You may have seen an octagon on the way here. A stop sign is an octagon."
4. With the child, count the eight sides of the octagon.
5. Tell the child, "All octagons have eight sides that are the same size."
6. Have the child sequence the octagons by size, starting with the smallest octagon on the left and progressing to the largest octagon on the right.

Octopus

ADULT PREPARATION:

1. Using the pattern, trace pattern and cut out an octopus with eight legs (detached) for each child.
2. Write the numbers 1–8 across the bottom edge of the front side of the paper octopus, in random order.
3. Number the legs 1–8.
4. Place the octopus, legs, and glue on the table.

PROCEDURES:

1. Tell the child that an octopus has eight legs.
2. Ask the child to identify each number written on the octopus.
3. Ask the child to select an octopus leg and identify the number on the leg.
4. The child then finds the same number on the octopus and glues the leg to that number.
5. Continue steps 3–4 until all legs have been matched and glued to the octopus.

DEVELOPMENTAL GOALS:

✄ To recognize numbers

✄ To improve fine motor skills

LEARNING OBJECTIVE:

Using a paper octopus, its detached legs, and glue, the child will identify the numbers 1–8.

MATERIALS:

Octopus and legs patterns (Appendix A33)
Construction paper
Scissors
Marker
White school glue

Ornaments

AGES: 3–5

**AGE: 2
(numbers 0–5)**

DEVELOPMENTAL GOALS:

- ✂ To improve identification of numbers
- ✂ To understand spatial relationships

LEARNING OBJECTIVE:

Using cards, ornaments, and a tree, the child will identify numbers and place ornaments on a tree according to spatial directions.

MATERIALS:

Assorted plastic or unbreakable holiday ornaments
Small artificial tree
Paper
Scissors
Permanent marker
Masking tape

ADULT PREPARATION:

1. Cut paper into 5" squares.
2. Draw an outline of a tree on each square.
3. Fill in the top of the tree with color on half the cards.
4. Fill in the lower half of the tree with color on the other half of the cards.
5. Write one number on each card.
6. Write numbers on pieces of masking tape to match the numbers on the cards and place the masking tape numbers on the ornaments.
7. Set up the small artificial tree on a table or on the floor.
8. Place the box of ornaments near the tree.
9. Place the cards face down on the table or floor.

continued

Ornaments continued

PROCEDURES:

The child will complete the following steps:

1. Select a card.
2. Identify the number on the card and then find the ornament with the same number.
3. When asked, identify whether the top or bottom half of the tree card is colored.
4. If the top half of the card is colored, place the ornament on the top half of the tree.
5. If the bottom half of the card is colored, place the ornaments on the bottom half of the tree.
6. Continue steps 1–5, using other cards.

VARIATIONS:

Hang objects on the tree to match the season or unit (objects may be purchased or made from paper). Some suggestions are apples for a food unit, shamrocks for a St. Patrick's Day unit, birds when studying rainforests, and butterflies when talking about spring.

Owls

AGES: 3–5
AGE: 2
(numbers 0–5)

DEVELOPMENTAL GOALS:

- ✂ To increase shape recognition
- ✂ To develop an understanding of number concepts

LEARNING OBJECTIVE:

Using paper owls and moons, the child will identify shapes and numbers and will count craters.

MATERIALS:

Owl pattern
(Appendix A34)
Paper
Markers, crayons, or
colored pencils
Scissors
Yellow construction
paper
Coffee can lid or other
round flat object

ADULT PREPARATION:

1. Trace pattern, then color and cut out 11 owls.
2. Write the numbers 0–10 on the owls.
3. Trace the round lid on yellow construction paper.
4. Cut 11 circles to represent moons.
5. Draw 0–10 ovals on each moon.
6. Set owls on the table in one row.
7. Set moons on the table in another row.

PROCEDURES:

1. Show the child the moons. Ask them, "What is the shape of the moon?"
2. If they do not answer correctly, tell them it is a circle when it is a full moon.
3. Tell the child that the moon has craters (holes) on its surface. Ask the child, "What is the shape of these craters?"
4. If they do not answer correctly, tell them that the shape is oval.
5. Tell the child, "Owls like to fly at night in the moonlight."
6. Ask the child to count the number of oval craters on each moon and to match it with the owl with the same number.

Penguins

ADULT PREPARATION:

1. Trace pattern, then color and cut out 12 penguins.
2. Draw a small triangle on the belly of one penguin, a medium triangle on another, and a large triangle on a third.
3. Draw small, medium, and large squares, circles, and rectangles on the remaining nine penguins.
4. Lay the 12 penguins on the table in random order.

PROCEDURES:

The child will complete the following steps:

1. Pick up the penguins with circles on their bellies.
2. Arrange them by size, from smallest to largest.
3. Repeat steps 1–2, finding and sequencing penguins with rectangles, squares, and triangles.

AGES: 3–5

AGE: 2 (only sort by shapes)

DEVELOPMENTAL GOALS:

✂ To enhance shape recognition

✂ To improve sorting skills

✂ To enhance the ability to sequence by size

LEARNING OBJECTIVE:

Using paper penguins, the child will identify shapes and will sort and sequence objects.

MATERIALS:

Penguin pattern (Appendix A35)
Paper
Crayons, markers, or colored pencils
Scissors

AGES: 3–5

DEVELOPMENTAL GOALS:

- ✂ To identify numbers
- ✂ To count money
- ✂ To develop eye-hand coordination

LEARNING OBJECTIVE:

Using piggy banks and pennies, the child will recognize numbers and will count money.

MATERIALS:

Plastic piggy banks with removable covers for easy access to coins
Pennies
Permanent marker
Plate

Piggy Banks

ADULT PREPARATION:

1. Using a marker, write one number on the side of each piggy bank.
2. Put pennies on a plate.
3. Line up the piggy banks in a row, in random order. The numbers on the banks should face the children.

PROCEDURES:

The child will complete the following steps:

1. Select one piggy bank and identify the number on its side.
2. Count out an equal number of pennies and deposit them in the piggy bank.
3. Repeat steps 1–2 until all piggy banks have received their deposits.

VARIATION:

Paper pigs and plastic or sticker money may be used.

Pizza

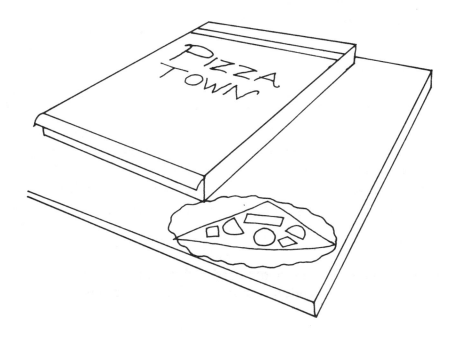

DEVELOPMENTAL
GOALS:

✄ To enhance
matching ability

✄ To identify shapes
and colors

✄ To recognize equal
amounts

LEARNING
OBJECTIVE:

Using a pizza box and
paper "pizza," the child
will recognize identical
shapes, colors, and
amounts.

MATERIALS:

Pizza boxes
Ruler
Markers
Scissors
Yellow poster board or
    tag board
Brown, green, gray, and
    white construction
    paper
Rubber cement
Plate

ADULT PREPARATION:

1. Ask a local pizza place for empty, clean, small pizza boxes.

2. Cut two circles out of yellow poster board to fit inside each
   pizza box.

3. Using a ruler and marker, divide the circles into eight equal slices
   (do not cut the slices apart).

4. Cut brown circles for pepperoni, narrow green rectangles for green
   peppers, gray half circles for mushrooms, and small white squares
   for onions.

5. Glue the "ingredients" on each pizza in an identical way (e.g., one
   slice of each pizza would have two pepperonis, two mushrooms,
   three bits of onion, and zero green peppers; another slice of each
   pizza would have one pepperoni, three mushrooms, two bits of
   onion, and three green peppers).

continued

Pizza continued

6. Glue one whole "pizza" inside a pizza box.
7. Cut the other pizza into slices.
8. Place the cut pizza slices on a plate.
9. Place the pizza box and the pizza slices on the table.

PROCEDURES:

The child will complete the following steps:

1. Pick a piece of pizza off the plate.
2. Look inside the pizza box and find the identical slice of pizza, by identifying and counting shapes and colors.
3. Set the pizza slice on the matching section of pizza inside the box.
4. Continue with steps 1–3 until all pizza slices are matched inside the box.

Note: The number of ingredients used will depend on the ability of the child. For younger children, start with less ingredients.

Porcupines

ADULT PREPARATION:

1. Trace pattern, then color and cut out 11 porcupines.
2. Write numbers 0–10 on the porcupines.
3. Place the corresponding number of dots on each porcupine to make the activity self-checking.
4. Place toothpicks in a bowl.
5. Set toothpicks and porcupines on the table.

PROCEDURES:

The child will complete the following steps:

1. Identify the number on a porcupine.
2. Count out the number of quills (toothpicks) that the porcupine needs (e.g., the porcupine with the number 4 needs four quills) and then place those "quills" on that porcupine.
3. Repeat steps 1–2 until all porcupines have the correct number of quills.

⊘ SAFETY PRECAUTION:

If the children are too young to handle toothpicks, use the wooden sticks that come with peg boards. Always supervise young children closely when they handle small objects.

AGES: 3–5

DEVELOPMENTAL GOALS:

- ✂ To develop number concepts
- ✂ To stimulate fine muscle development

LEARNING OBJECTIVE:

Using toothpicks and paper porcupines, the child will recognize numbers and count objects.

MATERIALS:

Porcupine pattern (Appendix A36)
Construction paper
Crayons, colored pencils, or markers
Scissors
Toothpicks
Bowl

Quails

AGES: 2¹/₂–5

DEVELOPMENTAL GOALS:

- ✂ To sequence by size
- ✂ To use left-to-right progression

LEARNING OBJECTIVE:

Using paper quails, the child will place them in left-to-right progression according to size.

MATERIALS:

Quail pattern
   (Appendix A37)
Construction paper
Scissors
Crayons, markers, or
   colored pencils

ADULT PREPARATION:

1. Trace patterns, then color and cut out quails of varying sizes.
2. Lay quails on the table in random order.

PROCEDURES:

Tell the child, "Baby quails follow their mother in a line. The largest quail is the mother. Find the mother and put her on your left." The child will complete the following steps:

1. Pick up the largest quail and put it on the right (with assistance, if necessary).
2. Line up the rest of the quails behind the mother quail, from smallest to largest.

Queens and Friends Matching

ADULT PREPARATION:

1. Select queens, jacks, and kings from the decks of cards.
2. Lay cards face down on table in rows.

PROCEDURES:

The child will complete the following steps:

1. Turn over two cards.
2. If the cards match, place them together, to one side, then take another turn.
3. If the cards do not match, return them to their facedown position. (The turn then passes to the next child.)
4. Repeat steps 1–3, taking turns with other children. The game ends when all of the cards have been matched.

Note: Start with four matches (eight cards) for younger children and then add more.

AGES: 3–5

DEVELOPMENTAL GOALS:

✂ To classify objects through matching

✂ To discriminate visually between objects that are similar but not identical

LEARNING OBJECTIVE:

Using the face cards from a deck of cards, the child will match objects.

MATERIALS:

Two decks of playing cards

Quilt Patterning

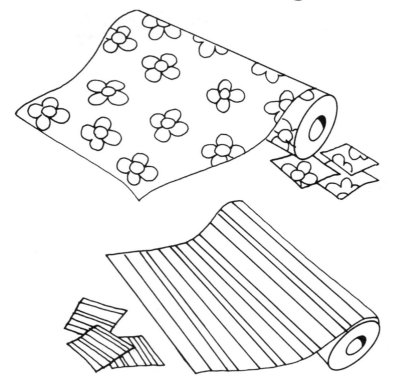

AGES: 4–5

DEVELOPMENTAL GOALS:

- ✂ To understand patterning
- ✂ To increase fine muscle development

LEARNING OBJECTIVE:

Using wallpaper squares, the child will create a patterned "quilt."

MATERIALS:

Pieces of wallpaper in different designs
Poster board
White school glue

ADULT PREPARATION:

1. Using two different patterns of wallpaper, cut 16—5" squares of each design.

2. Use eight squares of each type of wallpaper to form the quilt below.

3. Glue the wallpaper on a piece of poster board, using an AB pattern and a BA pattern for alternating rows, as shown:

A	B	A	B
B	A	B	A
A	B	A	B
B	A	B	A

continued

Quilt Patterning continued

4. Cut another piece of poster board the same size as the first.

5. Glue wallpaper squares on the poster board to make the first row and first column of a similarly patterned quilt.

6. Set the completed quilt (from steps 2–3) and the partly completed quilt on the table.

7. Place the wallpaper squares on the table.

PROCEDURES:

1. Show the child the completed wallpaper quilt.

2. Explain to the child that he or she will be making an identical quilt.

3. Ask the child to look at the first wallpaper square in the row.

4. Show the child the wallpaper squares on the table.

5. Tell the child that the different wallpaper designs will alternate.

6. The child will lay wallpaper squares on the poster board in rows, alternating AB and BA patterns.

Rabbits and Carrots

DEVELOPMENTAL GOALS:

- ✄ To identify numbers or shapes
- ✄ To recognize one-to-one correspondence
- ✄ To match similar objects

LEARNING OBJECTIVE:

Using paper carrots and rabbits, the child will recognize numbers or shapes and match corresponding items.

MATERIALS:

Rabbit and carrot patterns (Appendix A38)
White and orange paper
Crayons or markers
Scissors

ADULT PREPARATION:

1. Trace patterns and cut out equal numbers of rabbits and carrots, using white paper for the rabbits and orange paper for the carrots.
2. Draw same number or shape onto each pair of rabbits and carrots.
3. When using numbers with younger children, also draw the corresponding number of dots on each piece.
4. Lay rabbits and carrots on the table.

PROCEDURES:

The child will complete the following steps:

1. Place rabbits in a row.
2. Identify the number or shape on each rabbit and match it to the carrot with the same number or shape.

Rainbow

ADULT PREPARATION:

1. Trace rainbow pattern.
2. Using a copier make six sequential sizes of the pattern.
3. Cut out a graduated set of rainbow-color pieces for each child, using red, yellow, orange, blue, purple, and green construction paper.
4. Put each child's set of rainbow pieces in a resealable plastic bag.
5. Put individual bags of color strips and glue on the table.

PROCEDURES:

The child will complete the following steps:

1. Remove rainbow pieces from the plastic bag.
2. Identify the color of the largest piece.
3. Find the next largest piece and glue it to the first piece.
4. Find each successively smaller piece and glue it to the rainbow until all six colors of the rainbow are glued together in descending size order.

Note: Rainbows may be glued on a piece of construction paper.

AGES: 3–5

DEVELOPMENTAL GOALS:

✄ To sequence objects by size
✄ To identify colors

LEARNING OBJECTIVE:

Using paper rainbow pieces, the child will arrange and identify paper pieces by color and size.

MATERIALS:

Rainbow pattern (Appendix A39)
Red, yellow, orange, blue, purple, and green construction paper
Scissors
Resealable plastic bags
White school glue
Copier

Rockets

AGES: 3–5

**AGE: 2
(numbers 0–5)**

DEVELOPMENTAL GOALS:

- ✂ To recognize numbers
- ✂ To improve counting skills

LEARNING OBJECTIVE:

Using paper rockets, the child will recognize numbers and practice counting.

MATERIALS:

Rocket pattern (Appendix A40)
Paper
Crayons, markers, or colored pencils
Optional: foil star stickers

ADULT PREPARATION:

1. Trace pattern, then color and cut out 11 rockets.
2. Number the bases of the rockets from 0–10.
3. At the top of each rocket, place a number of dots (or star stickers) to correspond to the number on the base of the rocket.
4. Lay rocket bases on the table in a row.
5. Stack rocket tops on the table.

PROCEDURES:

The child will complete the following steps:

1. Identify numbers on the rocket bases.
2. Pick up the first rocket top from the stack and count the number of dots or stars on it.
3. Match that top to the base with the corresponding number by putting the rocket pieces together.
4. Repeat steps 2–3 until all rocket tops and bases are matched.

Rocks

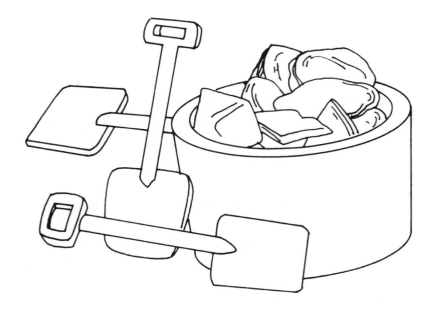

AGES: 3–5

DEVELOPMENTAL GOALS:

✂ To match colors

✂ To improve fine motor control

LEARNING OBJECTIVE:

Using rocks, shovel, plastic container, and color mats, the child will sort objects into sets by color.

MATERIALS:

Rocks
Small plastic shovel
Small plastic bucket
Construction paper

ADULT PREPARATION:

1. Collect rocks of various sizes and colors.
2. Cut out large circles of construction paper to make color mats. (Match the colors of the rocks to the colors of construction paper.)
3. Place rocks in a plastic bucket.
4. Set rocks, color mats, and shovel on table.

PROCEDURES:

The child will complete the following steps:

1. Identify the colors of the color mats.
2. Scoop rocks out of the container with the shovel, one at a time.
3. Sort through all rocks with the shovel, putting them on the construction paper circles that they match.

Shoe Matching

AGES: 3–5

DEVELOPMENTAL GOALS:

✂ To improve classification skills

✂ To acquire social skills

LEARNING OBJECTIVE:

Using shoes, the child will match like objects.

MATERIALS:

The children's shoes
Laundry basket

ADULT PREPARATION:

1. Place laundry basket in the center of an open area.

PROCEDURES:

1. Sit with children in a circle around the laundry basket.
2. Ask children to each take off one shoe and place it in the laundry basket.
3. Ask one child to select any shoe (except his or her own) from the laundry basket.
4. The child walks around the outside of the circle, looking at the other children's feet.
5. When the child finds the person wearing the matching shoe, he or she sets the shoe from the basket behind the sitting child.
6. The standing child continues walking around the outside of the circle.
7. The sitting child takes the shoe and walks after the first child.
8. The first child sits in the spot vacated by the second child.
9. The second child sets the shoe in the center of the circle, outside the laundry basket.
10. The second child selects a shoe from the laundry basket.
11. Steps 4–10 are repeated until all children have had a turn.
12. The child who takes the last turn may select a shoe from outside the basket so that he or she will have a turn to do steps 4–9.

94

Silverware Sorting

AGES: 3–5

DEVELOPMENTAL GOALS:

- ✂ To improve sorting skills
- ✂ To increase eye-hand coordination

LEARNING OBJECTIVE:

Using silverware and a divided silverware tray holder, the child will sort objects.

MATERIALS:

Assorted silverware
Divided plastic silverware tray
Dish towel

ADULT PREPARATION:

1. Collect silverware by sending home a letter to families to ask for unmatched pieces of flatware or by purchasing silverware from garage sales, thrift, or discount stores.
2. Place silverware on the table on a dish towel.
3. Set divided silverware tray on the table.

PROCEDURES:

The child will complete the following steps:
1. Find all the forks and put them in the same slot in the silverware tray.
2. Place all the spoons and knives in separate slots.

continued

Silverware Sorting continued

EXPANSION:

Children may count spoons, knives, and forks. They may also try to match silverware with identical patterns. Older children may lay out an ABC pattern with the silverware (e.g., spoon, fork, knife, spoon, fork, knife . . .).

VARIATION:

Make a placemat with silhouettes of a plate, cup, knife, fork, and spoon in the appropriate places. Have children match real plates, cups, and silverware to the silhouettes.

⚠ SAFETY PRECAUTION:

Use plastic or disposable plates and cups, and table knives with dull blades (or plastic flatware).

Snake Game

ADULT PREPARATION:

1. Trace pattern, then color and cut out snake.
2. Separate the head, tail, and squares of the snake by cutting them apart.
3. Add additional squares to make the snake longer, depending on the attention span of the children.
4. Make dots on each of the snake's squares (to represent the numbers 1–6). If making the snake longer by using additional squares, still make one to six dots on each to match the numbers on a die.
5. Set the dice and the snake head, tail, and dotted squares on the table.

PROCEDURES:

The first child taking a turn will complete the following steps:

1. Roll one die.
2. Count the number of dots on the die.
3. Find a square with the same number of dots and place it after the snake head. Other children will repeat steps 1–3. When all squares have been added to the snake, the tail may be put on.

VARIATION:

Color the snake squares in two or three separate colors. The child may create a pattern with the colors to complete the length of the snake.

AGES: 4–5

DEVELOPMENTAL GOALS:

✂ To count objects

✂ To become accustomed to taking turns

LEARNING OBJECTIVE:

Using snake puzzle pieces and dice, the child will count dots.

MATERIALS:

Snake pattern (Appendix A41)
Paper
Scissors
Markers
Dice

Snowmen

AGES: 3–5

DEVELOPMENTAL GOALS:

- ✕ To develop number concepts
- ✕ To sequence numbers correctly
- ✕ To become familiar with left-to-right progression

LEARNING OBJECTIVE:

Using paper snowmen and pom-poms or buttons, the child will sequence numbers from left to right, identify numbers, and use rational counting.

MATERIALS:

Snowman pattern (Appendix A42)
White paper
Scissors
Markers
Pom-poms or buttons
Bowl

ADULT PREPARATION:

1. Trace pattern and cut out 11 snowmen.
2. With markers, add facial features.
3. Write the numbers 0–10 on the snowmen.
4. Set the snowmen on the table in random order.
5. Place pom-poms or buttons in a bowl and place it on the table.

PROCEDURES:

The child will complete the following steps:

1. Identify the numbers on the snowmen and place them in sequential order from left to right, starting with zero.
2. Count out pom-poms or buttons to equal the number written on each snowman and place them on the snowman.

⬨ SAFETY PRECAUTION:

Maintain close supervision if the buttons or pom-poms are small. These items may present a choking hazard in young children.

Spiders

ADULT PREPARATION (DAY 1):

1. Cut out black circles to fit inside the box lid.
2. Pour one part white tempera paint and one part water into a small container.
3. Add a squirt of dish soap and mix well.
4. Place circle in box lid.
5. Add marbles and a spoon to the paint.
6. Cover table with newspaper.
7. Set materials on newspaper.

PROCEDURES (DAY 1):

The child will complete the following steps:

1. Wearing a smock, spoon marbles out of paint.
2. Carefully drain excess paint from spoon.
3. Place marbles on black circle in box lid.
4. Gently move box in order to roll marbles, making a trail of paint across the paper.
5. Replace marbles in the paint.
6. Repeat steps 1–5 to make more paint trails with marbles.
7. Set black circle (now containing a white "spider web") on a rack to dry.

ADULT PREPARATION (DAY 2):

1. Place white labels on each of the spider webs.
2. Using a marker, write a different number on each label.
3. Set the webs on the table.
4. Place plastic spiders in a bowl.

PROCEDURES (DAY 2):

The child will complete the following steps:

1. Identify the numbers on the spider webs.
2. Count and place spiders equal to the number on each web.

VARIATION:

If the concentration is on one number (such as a number of the week), the same number may be placed on each child's spider web.

AGES: 3–5

DEVELOPMENTAL GOALS:

✂ To recognize numbers

✂ To improve counting skills

✂ To practice one-to-one correspondence

LEARNING OBJECTIVE:

Using plastic spiders and paper webs, the child will place a specified number of spiders on each web.

MATERIALS:

Black construction paper
Scissors
Box lid
White tempera paint
Smock
Dish soap
Marbles
Small containers
Water
Spoons
White labels
Markers
Plastic spiders
Bowls

Teeth

AGES: 3–5

DEVELOPMENTAL GOALS:

- To identify numbers
- To refine small muscle movements

LEARNING OBJECTIVE:

Using a paper mouth and lima beans, the child will identify and match numbers.

MATERIALS:

Mouth pattern (Appendix A43)
Markers
Fine-tipped permanent marker
Large dry lima beans
Paper or tag board

ADULT PREPARATION:

1. Trace pattern on paper or tag board, then color and cut out large mouth.
2. Draw teeth in mouth.
3. Number the teeth in the mouth, starting with zero.
4. Using fine-tipped permanent marker, write numbers on large lima beans.
5. Set mouth and lima beans on table.

PROCEDURES:

The child will complete the following steps:

1. Identify one of the numbers on the teeth.
2. Find the identical number on a lima bean and place that bean on the tooth with that number.
3. Repeat steps 1–2 until all beans have been placed on teeth.

SAFETY PRECAUTION:

Supervise young children closely when using small objects such as lima beans.

Telephone

ADULT PREPARATION:

1. Take a photo of the class and an individual photo of each child; develop or print all photos.
2. Glue each photo on a separate piece of paper.
3. Write the child's name and home phone number under each child's individual picture.
4. Under the class picture, write "Our Phonebook."
5. Punch two or three holes along the same side of each page.
6. When dry, attach the pages with the metal rings, using the class picture page as the cover.
7. Set the phone book on the table, with two telephones. (Toy telephones or nonworking traditional or cell phones may be used.)

PROCEDURES:

1. Two children will sit at the table, each with a telephone.
2. The first child will look up the second child's page in the phone book.
3. The first child will identify the telephone numbers and press the correct number buttons on the phone.
4. The second child will answer the phone, and they may have a conversation.
5. The children will reverse roles and repeat steps 1–4.

Note: Check the center's policy regarding phone numbers before using this activity, because giving others access to the children's phone numbers may be viewed as a breach of confidentiality.

VARIATIONS:

Write the child's name and phone number on an index card. The child may look at his or her own phone number and practice calling home. If this activity is done at home, family members' pictures and phone numbers may be substituted for those of classmates.

T

AGES: 3–5

DEVELOPMENTAL GOALS:

- ✂ To recognize numbers
- ✂ To promote social skills
- ✂ To enhance eye-hand coordination

LEARNING OBJECTIVE:

Using a telephone and a class phone book, the child will dial classmates' phone numbers.

MATERIALS:

Class picture
Individual class pictures
Construction paper
Marker
Rubber cement
Hole puncher
Metal rings
Telephones

Ties

DEVELOPMENTAL GOALS:

- ✂ To match objects
- ✂ To identify similarities and differences

LEARNING OBJECTIVE:

Using ties, the child will put together similar objects.

MATERIALS:

Ties
Scissors
Thread
Needle or sewing
machine

ADULT PREPARATION:

1. Ask families for out-of-style or unused neckties.
2. Cut ties in three sections, each no longer than 12".
3. Using a thread and needle or sewing machine, make a hem in each of the unfinished ends of the tie pieces to prevent raveling.
4. Place tie pieces on the table or floor in random order.

PROCEDURES:

The child will complete the following steps:

1. Select a section of a tie.
2. Describe the fabric's design (stripes, dots, etc.).

continued

Ties continued

3. Look for other pieces of the same tie.

4. Put the tie pieces together: the wide pointed end, the middle piece with two straight ends, and then the narrow pointed end.

5. Repeat steps 1–4 until all tie pieces have been put back together.

Notes: Instead of hemming the ties, use iron-on hem tape. Do not apply iron directly to the fabric if silk ties are used, however; cover with a cloth before you iron. If real ties are not available, cut ties out of paper or wallpaper.

Train

AGES: 3–5

DEVELOPMENTAL GOALS:

- ✄ To improve number recognition
- ✄ To sequence numbers
- ✄ To use ordinal numbers

LEARNING OBJECTIVE:

Using a train set, the child will sequence the train cars by number.

MATERIALS:

Interlocking train set
Construction paper
Markers
Masking tape
Scissors

ADULT PREPARATION:

1. Cut construction paper into small squares or other shapes.
2. Write a number on each squares, starting with zero. (The corresponding number of dots may also be drawn on each square.)
3. Tape the piece of paper numbered zero to the train engine.
4. Tape the other numbers on the remaining train pieces.
5. If there is a caboose, it will receive the highest number.
6. Place the train on the table or floor with the cars separated and set down in random order.

PROCEDURES:

1. Ask the child to identify the numbers on the train pieces.
2. Tell the child that the object is to place the train cars in order behind the engine.
3. Place the engine in front of the child. Ask, "Which car will be placed first behind the engine?" The child may need guidance to select the car numbered one and attach it behind the engine.
4. Ask the child, "Which car will go second?"
5. After the child attaches the car bearing the number two, ask the child, "Which car will go third?"
6. Repeat the ordinal question and have the child continue attaching the train cars in sequential order.

Note: A paper cutout of a train may be substituted for a toy train.

EXPANSION:

If the train has open cars, the child may identify the number on the car and then count out a corresponding number of plastic animals, people, or other objects to place in the train car.

Turtles

ADULT PREPARATION:

1. Trace pattern, then color and cut out five turtles.
2. Draw a circle on the shell of the first turtle, an oval on the second, a triangle on the third, a rectangle on the fourth, and a square on the fifth.
3. Draw additional circles, ovals, triangles, rectangles, and squares on construction paper and cut out.
4. Set turtles on the table.
5. Place shapes on the table in a bowl.

PROCEDURES:

The child will complete the following steps:

1. Identify the shape on each turtle.
2. Select a shape from the bowl.
3. Identify the shape and put it on a matching turtle's shell.
4. Repeat steps 2–3 until all shapes have been sorted.

AGES: 2–5

DEVELOPMENTAL GOALS:

- ✄ To identify shapes
- ✄ To sort shapes into sets

LEARNING OBJECTIVE:

Using paper turtles and shapes, the child will identify and sort shapes.

MATERIALS:

Turtle pattern (Appendix A44)
Construction paper
Marker, crayons, or colored pencils
Scissors
Bowl

U.S. Flag

DEVELOPMENTAL GOALS:

✂ To improve patterning skills

✂ To identify the flag of the United States

LEARNING OBJECTIVE:

Using construction paper stripes and foil stars, the child will create an American flag.

MATERIALS:

U.S. flag
Red, white, and blue construction paper
Scissors
White school glue
Silver foil star stickers

ADULT PREPARATION:

1. Cut seven red and six white strips of paper 3/4" thick and 12" long, for each child.

2. Cut a 4" by 5" blue rectangle for each child.

3. Set strips, rectangles, 9" by 12" sheets of blue construction paper, stars, and glue on the table.

4. Put the flag on the table or hang it where it is easy to see.

PROCEDURES:

1. Ask the child to identify the colors of the flag.

2. Ask the child which color stripe is at the top of the flag.

3. The child will glue a red stripe at the top of the sheet of blue construction paper.

continued

U.S. Flag continued

4. The child will then glue a white stripe beneath the red stripe.
5. The child will create an AB pattern by alternating red and white stripes, ending with a red stripe.

6. The child will glue the 4" by 5" blue rectangle in the top left corner.
7. The child will peel the star stickers and place them on the blue rectangle.

Note: Older children may count to 50 as they place the stars. Younger children may place as many star stickers as their attention span warrants.

Umbrellas

DEVELOPMENTAL GOALS:

✂ To recognize numbers

✂ To develop counting skills

LEARNING OBJECTIVE:

Using paper raindrops and umbrellas, the child will identify numbers and practice counting.

MATERIALS:

Umbrella and raindrop patterns (Appendix A45)
Construction paper
Markers
Scissors
Table
Bowl

ADULT PREPARATION:

1. Trace pattern and cut out 11 umbrellas.
2. Trace pattern and cut out 55 raindrops.
3. Number the umbrellas 0–10.
4. Set umbrellas on the table in random order.
5. Place raindrops in a bowl on the table.

PROCEDURES:

The child will complete the following steps:

1. Identify the number on an umbrella.
2. Count out that many raindrops and place on the corresponding umbrella.
3. Repeat steps 1–2 until all umbrellas have the raindrops to match their numbers.

VARIATION:

Instead of numbers, glue shapes on the umbrellas and raindrops. Ask the child to identify the shapes on the umbrellas. Then ask the child to choose matching shapes from an assortment of parquetry blocks (small wooden blocks in basic shapes) or foam shapes, and to place them on corresponding shapes on the umbrellas.

Unicorns

ADULT PREPARATION:

1. Trace patterns and cut out 5–10 unicorns in a number of different colors.
2. Cut the horn and the tail off each unicorn.
3. Set unicorn pieces on the table in random order.

PROCEDURES:

The child will complete the following steps:
1. Select a unicorn body, identifying its color.
2. Sort through other pieces to find the same-color horn and tail.
3. Put the unicorn together.
4. Repeat steps 1–3 until all unicorns are put together.

VARIATION:

Using a toy unicorn and a princess doll, practice spatial relationships (ask the child to place the princess *on* the back of the unicorn, to place the princess *in front of* the unicorn, to place the princess *behind* the unicorn, and so on).

AGES: 2½–5

DEVELOPMENTAL GOALS:

- ✂ To develop classification skills
- ✂ To recognize colors

LEARNING OBJECTIVE:

Using paper unicorn bodies, tails, and horns, the child will match like objects.

MATERIALS:

Unicorn pattern (Appendix A46)
Construction paper in several colors
Scissors

Valentine Matching

AGES: 3–5

DEVELOPMENTAL GOALS:

✂ To discriminate between objects that are the same and different

✂ To take turns

LEARNING OBJECTIVE:

Using valentine cards, the child will pair valentines that are alike.

MATERIALS:

Box of children's valentines (make sure there are duplicates)

ADULT PREPARATION:

1. Sort valentines, putting duplicates in separate stacks.
2. Select only two of each type.
3. Lay the valentine pairs face down on the table in random order.

PROCEDURES:

Two children may play this matching game:

1. The first child will turn over two cards.
2. If the cards match, the child will place them to one side. If the cards do not match, the child will turn them face down again.
3. It is then the next child's turn; he or she repeats steps 1–2.
4. The children continue taking turns until all the matches have been found.

Note: For younger children, start with only four matches (eight cards). Add more cards as the children's attention span increases.

continued

110

Valentine Matching continued

EXPANSION:

Using all of the valentines, sort them into sets and then create patterns with the cards.

VARIATION:

Provide newspapers or newspaper inserts containing duplicates of several different valentine advertisements. Have the child find the identical ads, then cut and glue them on a sheet of paper.

Van

AGES: 3–5

AGE: 2
(numbers 0–5)

DEVELOPMENTAL GOALS:

- ✂ To recognize numbers
- ✂ To enhance counting skills

LEARNING OBJECTIVE:

Using a paper van and photos of persons, the child will recognize a number and count the corresponding number of persons.

MATERIALS:

Van pattern
   (Appendix A47)
Construction paper
Scissors
Magazines
White school glue
Marker

ADULT PREPARATION:

1. Cut out one van for each child, from construction paper.
2. Select a number to write on the van, such as the number of the week or the child's age.
3. Cut photos of people out of magazines.
4. Place van, photos, and glue on the table.

PROCEDURES:

The child will complete the following steps:

1. Identify the number on the van.
2. Count the corresponding number of photos of persons and glue them on the van.

Note: You may want to have the child cut the photos out of the magazines.

Vests

ADULT PREPARATION:

1. Trace pattern and cut out a matching vest front and back from each wallpaper design.
2. Set vest pieces on the table in random order.

PROCEDURE:

1. The child will match each vest front with a vest back cut from the same wallpaper.

EXPANSION:

Write numbers on the front of the vest. Have the child identify each number and place the corresponding number of buttons on each vest.

VARIATION:

Use solid-color paper to make the front of the vest and draw geometric shapes on it. Have the child identify the shape and then place similar parquetry blocks on the vest.

AGES: 2–5

DEVELOPMENTAL GOALS:

- ✂ To match objects
- ✂ To discriminate between similar objects

LEARNING OBJECTIVE:

Using paper vest pieces, the child will match like objects.

MATERIALS:

Vest pattern
   (Appendix A48)
Wallpaper in a variety
   of designs
Scissors

Watermelon Slices

AGES: 3–5

DEVELOPMENTAL GOALS:

- ✄ To enhance number recognition
- ✄ To develop counting skills

LEARNING OBJECTIVE:

Using watermelon seeds and paper watermelon slices, the child will count and will identify numbers.

MATERIALS:

Watermelon slice pattern (Appendix A49)
Paper
Markers
Scissors
Bowl
Watermelon seeds or black beans

ADULT PREPARATION:

1. Trace pattern, then color and cut out 11 watermelon slices.
2. Write a number (0–10) on the rind of each watermelon slice.
3. Set watermelon seeds in a bowl. (If seeds are unavailable, use black beans.)
4. Set watermelon slices on the table in random order.

PROCEDURES:

The child will complete the following steps:

1. Identify the number on each watermelon slice.
2. Count out that many seeds and place them on the watermelon slice.
3. Repeat steps 1–2 until all watermelon slices have the appropriate number of seeds.

EXPANSION:

Ask the child to place watermelon slices in numerical sequence from 0–10.

SAFETY PRECAUTION:

Supervise children closely when they are handling small objects.

114

Western Wagons

ADULT PREPARATION:

1. Trace pattern, then color and cut out 5–10 western wagons and covers.
2. Cut base and cover apart.
3. Cut geometric shapes out of black construction paper, in duplicate pairs.
4. Glue a different shape on each wagon cover.
5. Glue matching shapes on the wagon bases.
6. Lay wagon bases on the table in a row, in random order.
7. Lay wagon covers in a row beneath the wagon bases, in random order.

PROCEDURES:

The child will complete the following steps:
1. Identify the shapes on the wagon bases.
2. Match the pairs of shapes by putting the wagon cover above the wagon base of the same geometric shape.

VARIATION:

Write numbers on the wagon covers and draw dots on the bases to match the corresponding numbers. Have the child identify the number on the cover and count the dots on each base until the corresponding base is found for each cover.

AGES: 2–5

DEVELOPMENTAL GOALS:

✂ To identify shapes
✂ To match shapes
✂ To develop an understanding one-to-one correspondence

LEARNING OBJECTIVE:

Using paper bases and covers for western wagons, the child will identify and match geometric shapes.

MATERIALS:

Western wagon base and cover patterns (Appendix A50)
Paper
Markers and crayons
Black construction paper
Scissors
Rubber cement

Women Matching

AGES: 3–5

DEVELOPMENTAL GOALS:

- ✄ To match like objects
- ✄ To observe similarities and differences
- ✄ To acquire social skills

LEARNING OBJECTIVE:

Using photos of women, the child will match like objects.

MATERIALS:

Duplicate newspapers or magazines
Scissors
Rubber cement
Construction paper

ADULT PREPARATION:

1. Cut duplicate photos of women out of newspapers or magazines.
2. Cut construction paper into 4" squares.
3. Glue the pictures of women on the construction paper squares, making pairs of photo cards.
4. Lay one photo from each pair face up on the table, in a row.
5. Place the other pictures in a stack, face down.

PROCEDURES:

1. Two children will sit at the table.
2. The first child will take the first card from the stack, look at the row of photos, and find the matching photo.
3. The first child will lay the photo from the stack on top of its match in the row.
4. The second child then takes the top card from the stack and repeats the process.
5. The children alternate turns until all the photo cards have a match.

Wrapped Box Matching

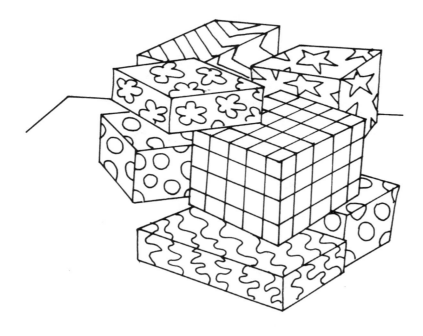

AGES: 3–5

DEVELOPMENTAL GOALS:

✂ To match objects

✂ To follow directions

✂ To understand spatial terms

LEARNING OBJECTIVE:

Using wrapped boxes, the child will match objects and follow spatial directions.

MATERIALS:

Wrapping paper in several different designs
Empty boxes
Scissors
Tape

ADULT PREPARATION:

1. Send a letter home requesting that families send in small empty boxes.

2. Wrap pairs of boxes in identical wrapping paper. (The boxes in each pair do not need to be the same size; they simply need to be wrapped in matching paper.)

3. Place boxes on the table or floor, all mixed together.

PROCEDURES:

1. Have the children sit in a circle around the wrapped boxes.

2. Hand each child a wrapped box, leaving the duplicate wrapped boxes in the center.

3. Have each child look through the center pile to find the box that matches his or her own.

continued

117

Wrapped Box Matching continued

VARIATION:

The adult will place one box of each matched pair throughout the classroom. The adult will then put the remaining boxes in the center of the circle. Each child will select a different wrapped box from the center of the circle. Then each child will look around the room for the box that matches the one he or she is holding.

X Marks

ADULT PREPARATION:

1. Collect maps with symbols written on them to designate areas. Park maps work well because they have symbols of picnic tables, camping, water, trails, and restrooms.
2. Laminate the maps.
3. Slightly dampen a piece of cloth.
4. Set cloth, map, and a dry erase marker on the table.

PROCEDURES:

1. Identify the symbols on the map for the child.
2. On a plain sheet of paper, show the child how to write an X.
3. Have the child practice making an X, using a marker.
4. Explain to the child that people mark an X on a treasure map to remind them where they have buried their treasure.
5. Ask the child to draw an X on the map with the dry erase marker.
6. Give the child directions using the spatial terms *under, over, on, in, beside, between*, and *above* (e.g., "Put the X *under* the picnic table").
7. When the child has finished following directions, he or she may erase the Xs with the damp cloth.

Note: Maps may be printed from the Internet.

AGES: 4–5

DEVELOPMENTAL GOALS:

✂ To develop an understanding of spatial concepts
✂ To follow directions
✂ To enhance eye-hand coordination

LEARNING OBJECTIVE:

Using a map and a marker, the child will follow spatial directions.

MATERIALS:

Map
Lamination
Dry erase marker
Damp cloth
Paper

Xylophone

AGES: 3¹/₂–5

DEVELOPMENTAL GOALS:

✂ To sequence by size

✂ To use left-to-right progression

LEARNING OBJECTIVE:

Using a paper xylophone, the child will identify the colors of rectangles while gluing them in sequential order to match a toy xylophone.

MATERIALS:

Construction paper in two distinct colors
Scissors
White school glue
Toy xylophone

ADULT PREPARATION:

1. Cut one color of construction paper into 1"-wide strips.
2. Cut the strips into 8 lengths: Match those lengths to the size of the 8 keys on the toy xylophone. Make a set containing one rectangle of each length, for each child.
3. Cut a 9" by 9" square of the other color of construction paper for each child.
4. Lay the toy xylophone, rectangles, squares, and glue on the table.

PROCEDURES:

The child will complete the following steps:

1. Identify the shape (rectangle) of the xylophone keys.
2. Look at the toy xylophone and choose the rectangle that matches the size of the largest key on the toy.

continued

Xylophone continued

3. Glue that large rectangle on the left side of the paper.

4. Glue the other seven rectangles on the paper in decreasing size, from largest to smallest, left to right, matching the sizes of the keys on the toy xylophone.

Note: If the toy xylophone has eight different colors of keys, match the rectangles by color and size.

Yarn Numbers

DEVELOPMENTAL GOALS:

✂ To improve number recognition

✂ To develop fine motor skills

LEARNING OBJECTIVE:

Using construction paper, glue, cotton swabs, and yarn, the child will decorate and identify a number.

MATERIALS:

Construction paper
Marker
Scissors
White school glue
Milk caps
Cotton swabs
Yarn of various colors
Plate

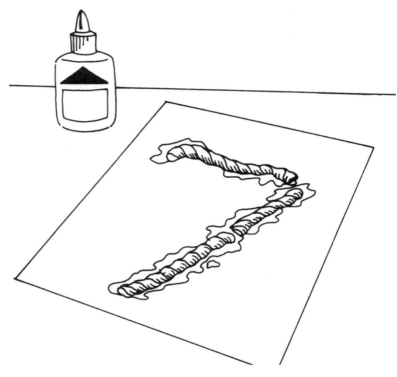

ADULT PREPARATION:

1. Write a number on a piece of 9" by 13" construction paper for each child. The number may fill the paper.

2. Cut 1" lengths of yarn and place them on a plate.

3. Pour glue into milk caps.

4. Place cotton swabs and glue on the table.

5. Set the papers with numbers and the plate of yarn on the table.

PROCEDURES:

The child will complete the following steps:

1. Identify the number on the paper.

2. Outline the number with glue, using a cotton swab.

3. Place pieces of yarn on the glue.

4. After the glue is dry, trace the yarn-covered number with a finger.

Note: For younger children use a 5" x 7" piece of paper to accommodate their shorter attention span.

Yogurt Containers

ADULT PREPARATION:

1. Send a note home asking families to send in clean, empty yogurt containers.
2. Make sure there are at least two of each type of cup.
3. Place one of each pair of containers in a row on the table.
4. Stack the other containers and put them on the table.

PROCEDURES:

The child will complete the following steps:

1. Identify the different types of fruit pictured on the containers set out in a row. .
2. Take the top container from the stack.
3. Identify the picture on the container and set it on the table with the identical yogurt container.
4. Repeat steps 2–3 until all of the containers have been placed in pairs.

Note: If different brands of yogurt are used the pictures of the same fruit may be different

AGES: 2–5

DEVELOPMENTAL GOALS:

- ✂ To promote classification by matching objects
- ✂ To discriminate between objects that are alike and different

LEARNING OBJECTIVE:

Using various yogurt cups, the child will sort objects based on common characteristics.

MATERIALS:

Clean, empty yogurt containers

Yo-yos

AGES: 3½–5

DEVELOPMENTAL GOALS:

✄ To measure length

✄ To identify colors

✄ To sort by color

LEARNING OBJECTIVE:

Using yo-yos and paper circles, the child will measure string and will sort and identify colors.

MATERIALS:

Yo-yos in an assortment of sizes and colors
Construction paper
Scissors
Masking tape

ADULT PREPARATION:

1. Cut an assortment of 3" circles to match the colors of the yo-yos.
2. Lay the circles in a row on the table.
3. Put the yo-yos on the table.

PROCEDURES:

The child will complete the following steps:

1. Identify the colors of the circles on the table.
2. Sort the yo-yos by color, placing them with the paper circles of the same color.
3. Unwind the string of a yo-yo.
4. Tape the string in a straight line on the table, with adult assistance.
5. Take paper circles and lay them along the length of the yo-yo string, measuring the string by the number of circles used.
6. Watch as adult writes on a piece of masking tape how many circles equal the length of the yo-yo's string.
7. Place the numbered tape on top of the yo-yo.
8. Pull up the string and wind it around the yo-yo.
9. Repeat steps 3–8 with other yo-yos.
10. When finished, look at the numbers on the yo-yos.
11. When asked, identify which string is longest and which string is shortest.

124

Zebras

ADULT PREPARATION:

1. Trace pattern and cut out 10 or more zebras.
2. Draw varying numbers of stripes on each zebra.

PROCEDURES:

The child will complete the following steps:

1. Count the stripes on each zebra.
2. Sequence the zebras from the one with the fewest stripes to the one with the most stripes.

Note: You may give the child zebras without stripes and have the child count and place the correct number of stripes on each zebra.

AGES: 3–5

DEVELOPMENTAL GOALS:

✄ To develop counting ability

✄ To sequence by amount

LEARNING OBJECTIVE:

Using paper zebras, the child will count and will sequence by stripes.

MATERIALS:

Zebra pattern (Appendix A51)
Paper
Markers
Scissors

DEVELOPMENTAL GOALS:

✂ To recognize numbers

✂ To improve counting skills

LEARNING OBJECTIVE:

Using paper zinnias, paper stems, and flower seeds, the child will count and identify numbers.

MATERIALS:

Zinnia and stem patterns (Appendix A52)
Paper
Crayons, markers, or colored pencils
Scissors
Seeds
White school glue

Zinnias

ADULT PREPARATION:

1. Trace patterns, then color and cut out 11 zinnias and stems.
2. Number the stems from 0–10.
3. Glue seeds on a zinnia to correspond to each of the numbers on the stems.
4. Place the stems on the table in a row, in random order.
5. Place the zinnias on the table in a row under the stems, in random order.

PROCEDURES:

The child will complete the following steps:

1. Identify the number on each stem.
2. Count the number of seeds on each zinnia.
3. Match the number on each stem to the corresponding number of seeds on a zinnia by placing the matching stem under each zinnia.
4. Continue steps 2–3 until all zinnias have their stems.

Note: Zinnia seeds are very small and difficult for small children to handle, so larger seeds (sunflower, watermelon) or black beans should be used instead.

VARIATION:

Take photos of a zinnia and a zucchini and make at least 10 copies of each picture. Have the child make an AB pattern (e.g., zinnia, zucchini, zinnia, zucchini).

 SAFETY PRECAUTION:

Supervise children closely when handling small seeds.

Zippers

ADULT PREPARATION:

1. Send a letter home asking families to save the zippers from discarded clothing.
2. Put buttons in a bowl and place it on the table.
3. Place zippers on the table.

PROCEDURES:

The child will complete the following steps:

1. Identify the colors of the zippers.
2. Sort zippers by color.
3. Select a zipper.
4. Lay buttons along the length of the zipper.
5. Watch as adult records how many buttons equal the length of the zipper. The number is written on masking tape and then placed on the zipper.
6. Repeat steps 3–5 until all zippers have been measured.
7. Identify which zipper is the shortest and which one is the longest.

AGES: 4–5

DEVELOPMENTAL GOALS:

✂ To classify objects
✂ To measure length

LEARNING OBJECTIVE:

Using zippers and buttons, the child will sort and measure zippers.

MATERIALS:

Zippers
Buttons—identical size
Bowl
Masking tape
Permanent marker

Appendix

A1.   SQUIRREL

A2. ACORN

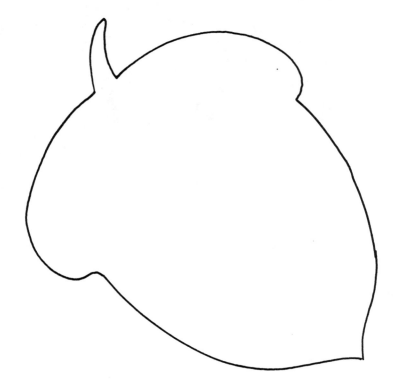

A3. ALLIGATOR

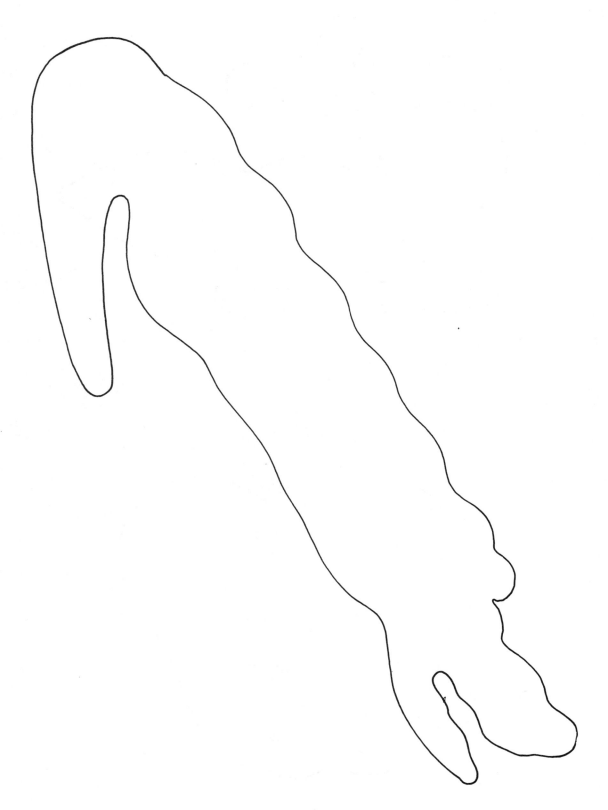

A4. ANT

A5. APPLE

A6. BANANA TREE AND BANANA BUNCHES

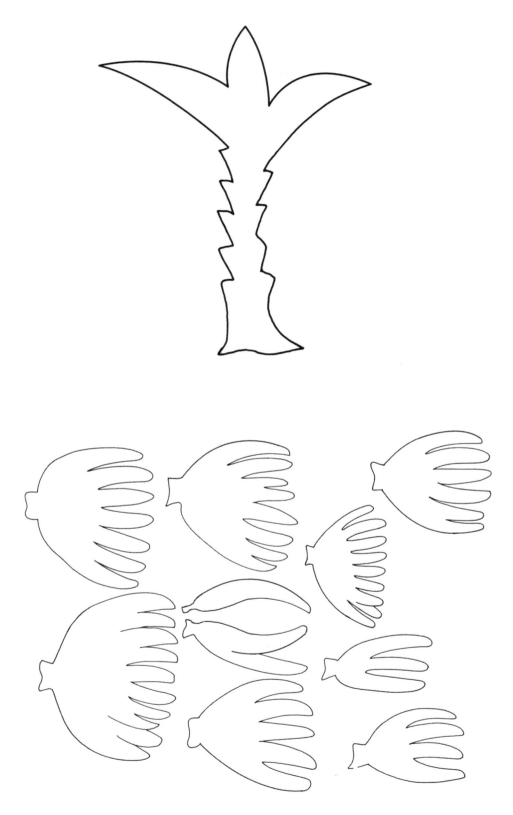

A7. BEE AND BEEHIVE

A8. BIRD AND NEST

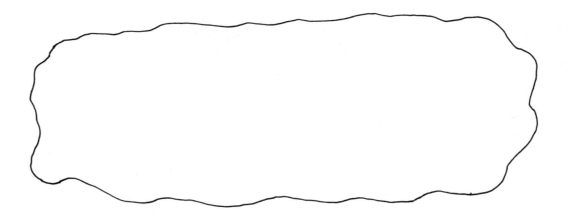

A9. CHICKEN AND EGG

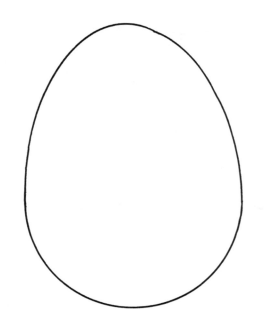

A10. CLOWN COLLAR

A11. DALMATIAN AND FIRE HYDRANT

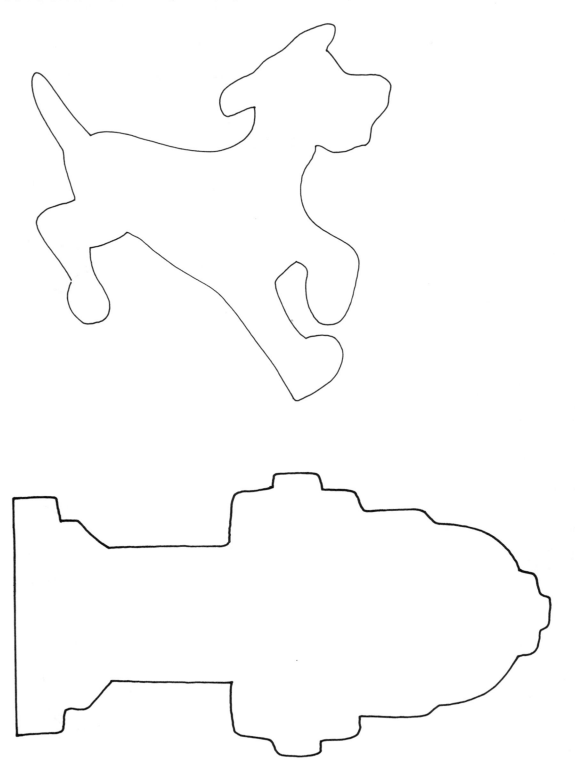

A12. DOCTOR'S BAG

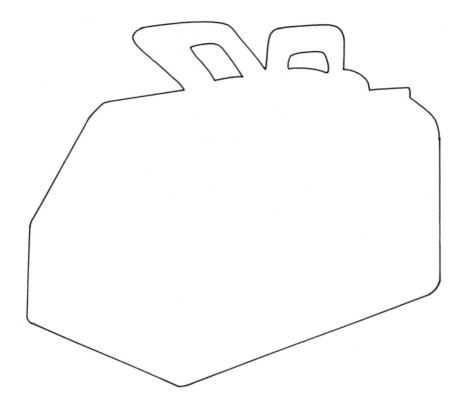

A13. DOG AND BONE

A14. ELEPHANT

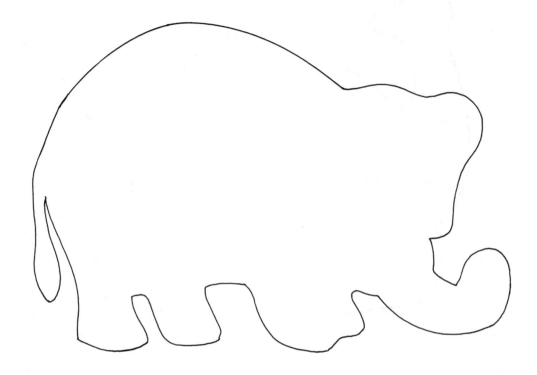

A15. FISH

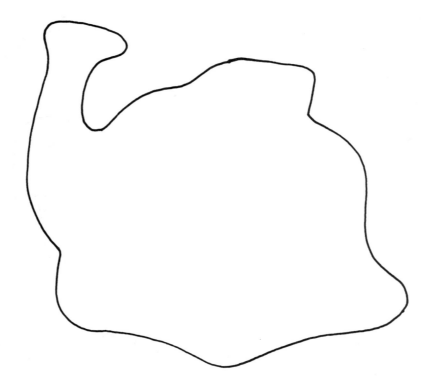

A16. GINGERBREAD MAN

A17. GIRAFFE

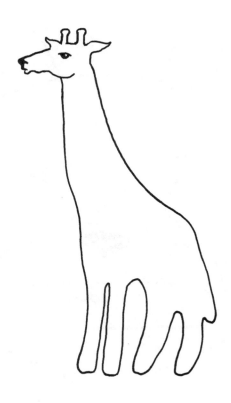

A18. GOAT HEAD

A19. GROUNDHOG

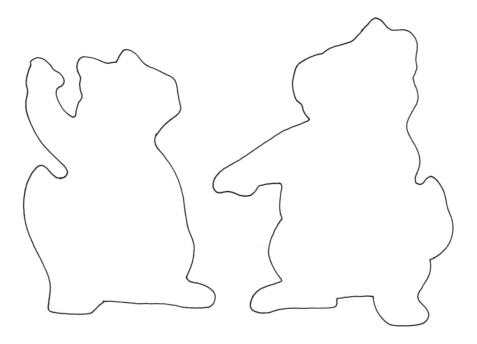

A20. HOT AIR BALLOON AND BASKET

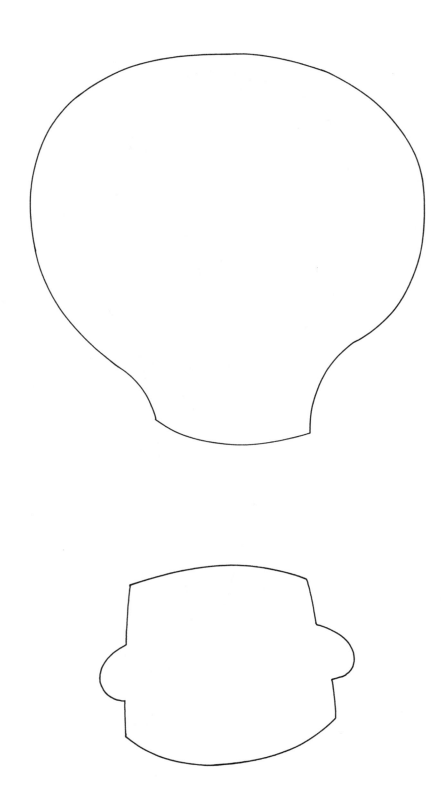

A21. ICE CREAM CONE

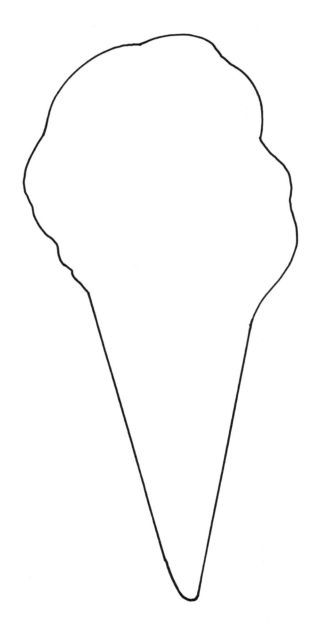

A22. IGLOO

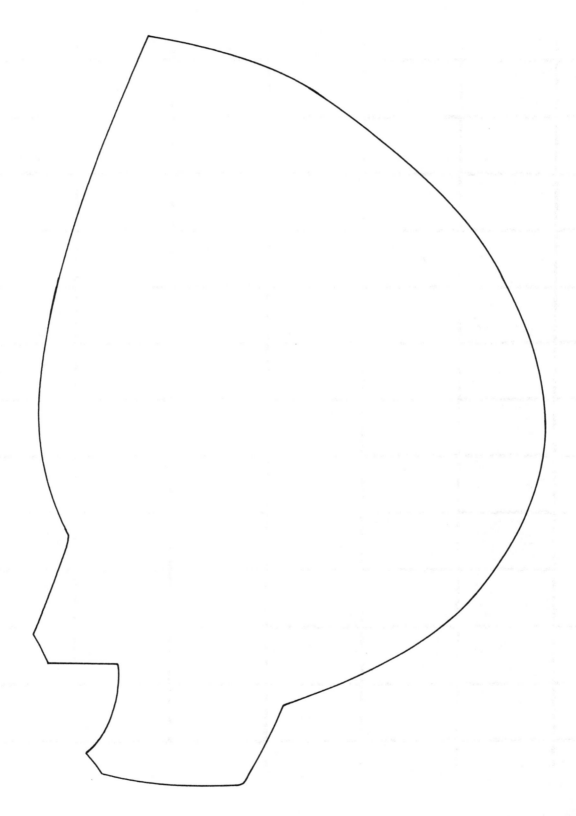

A23. GRAPH

A24. KANGAROO AND JOEY

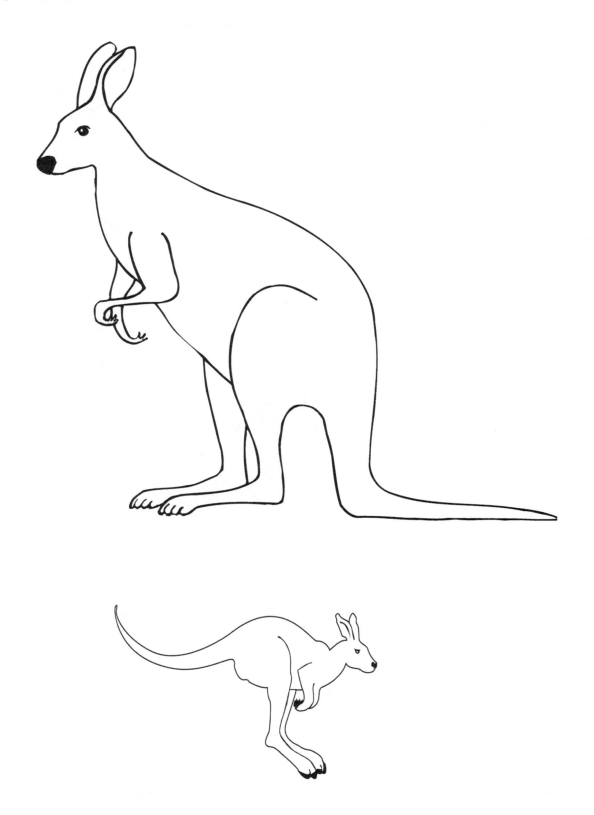

A25. CAR

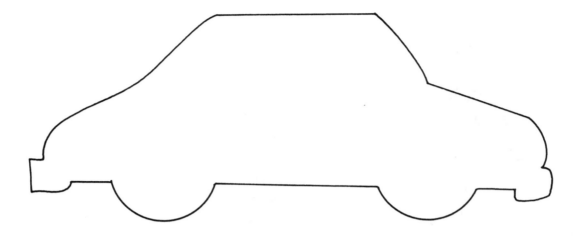

A26. KITE

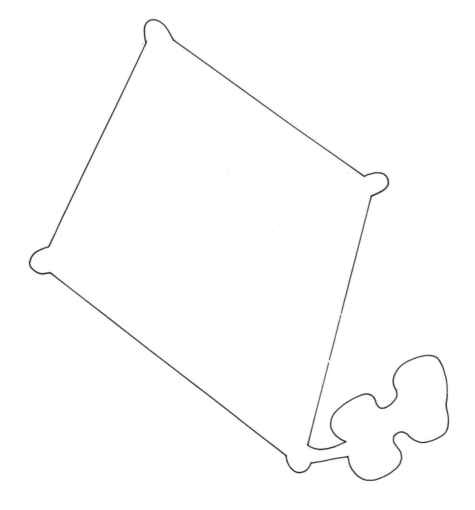

A27. TREE AND KOALA

A28. LADYBUG AND LEAF

A29. LEPRECHAUN'S POT

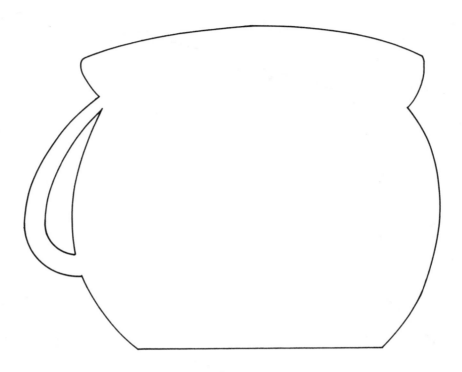

A30. MAILBOX AND FLAG

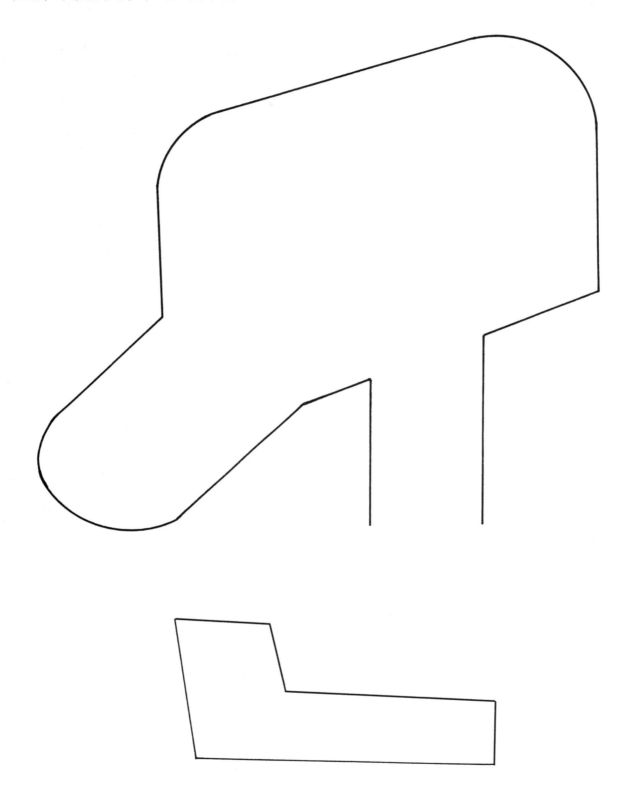

A31. MONKEY AND BANANA

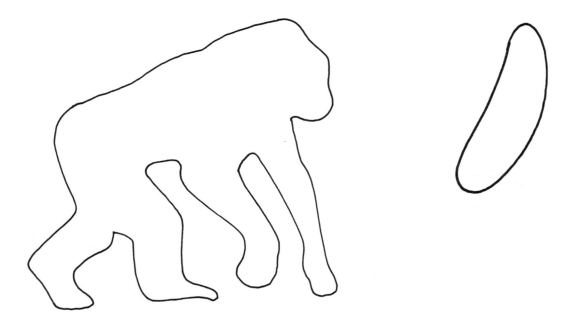

A32. OCTAGON

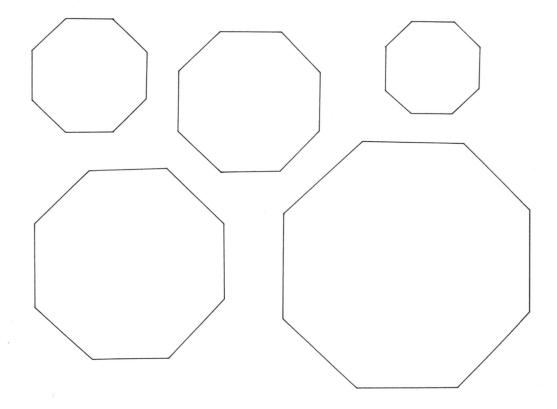

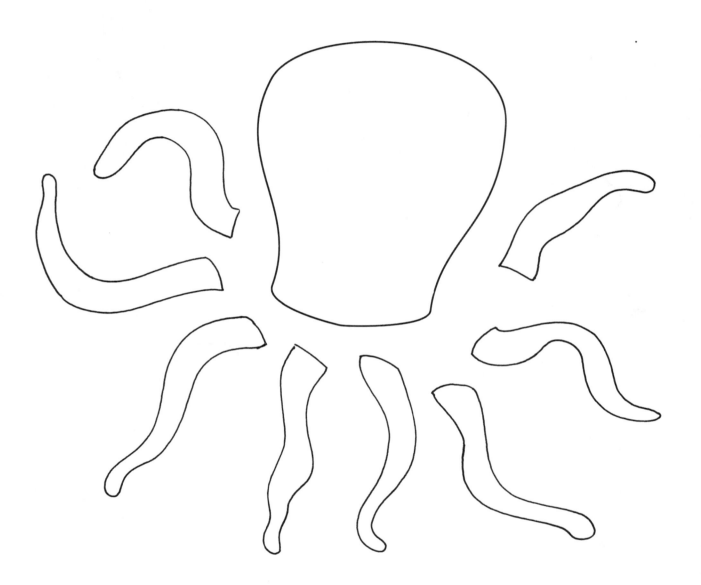

A34. OWL

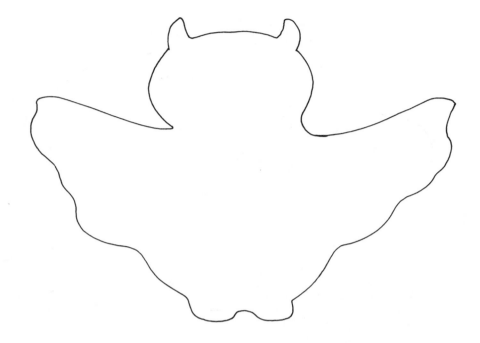

A35. PENGUIN

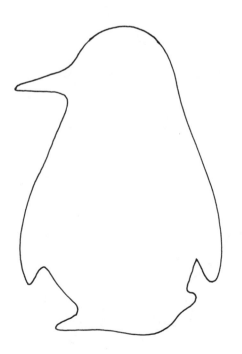

A36. PORCUPINE

A37. QUAIL

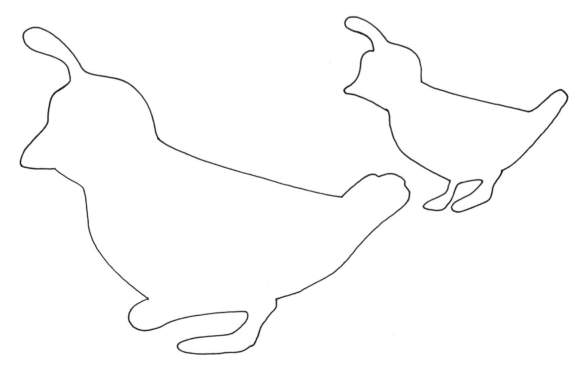

A38. RABBIT AND CARROT

A39. RAINBOW

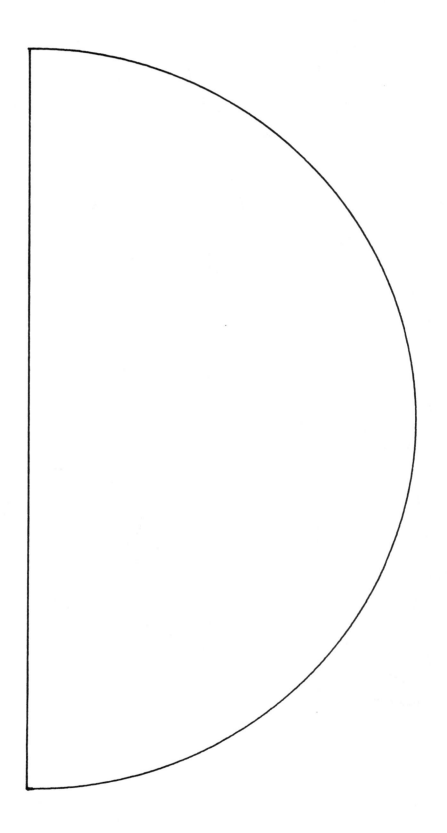

A40. ROCKET

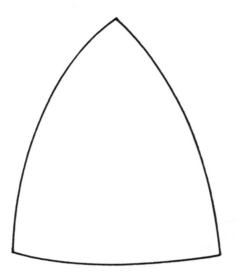

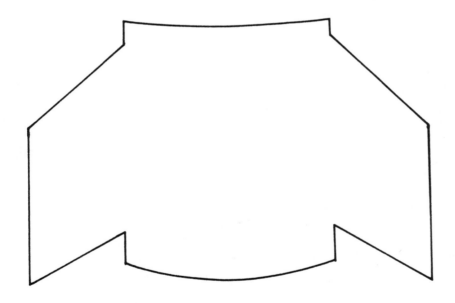

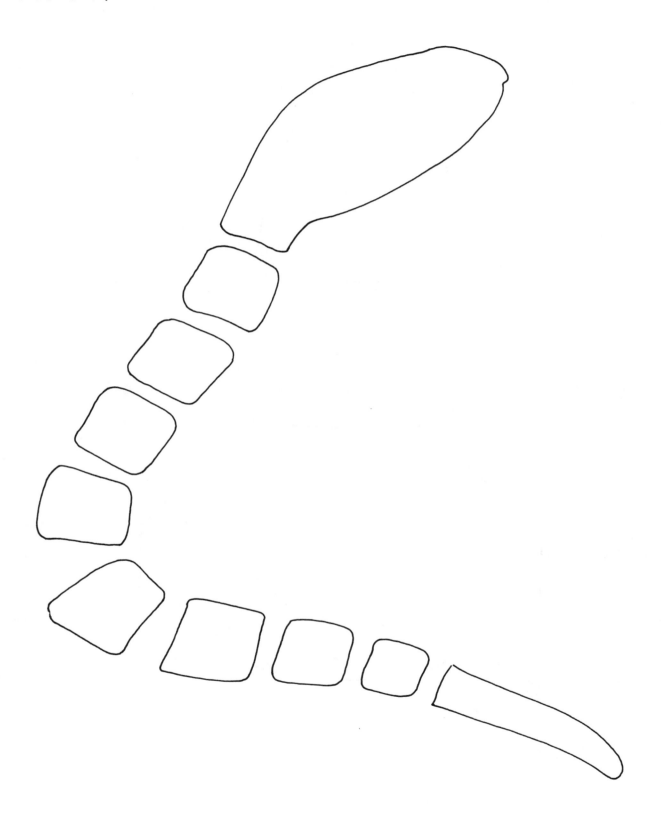

A42. SNOWMAN

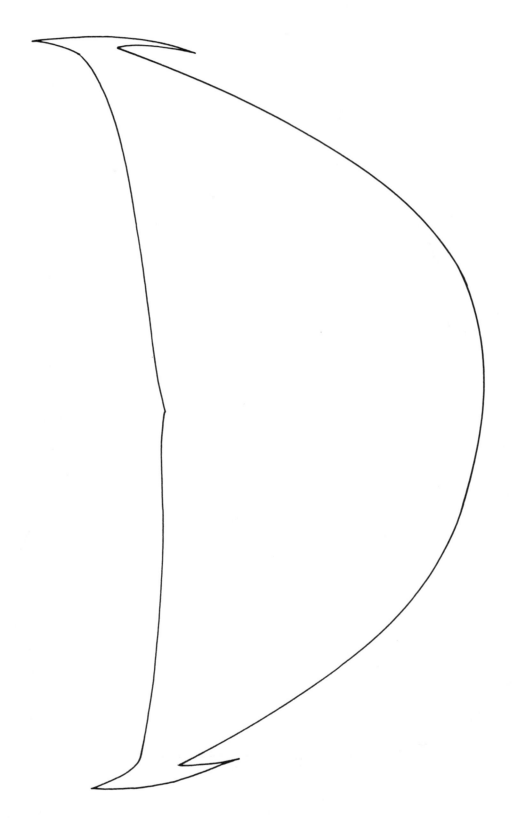

A44. TURTLE

A45. UMBRELLA AND RAINDROP

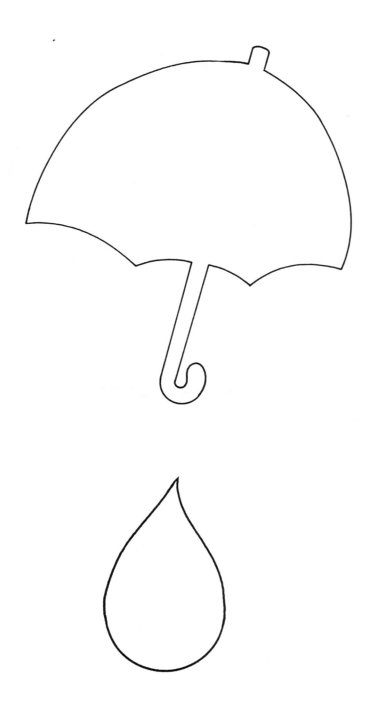

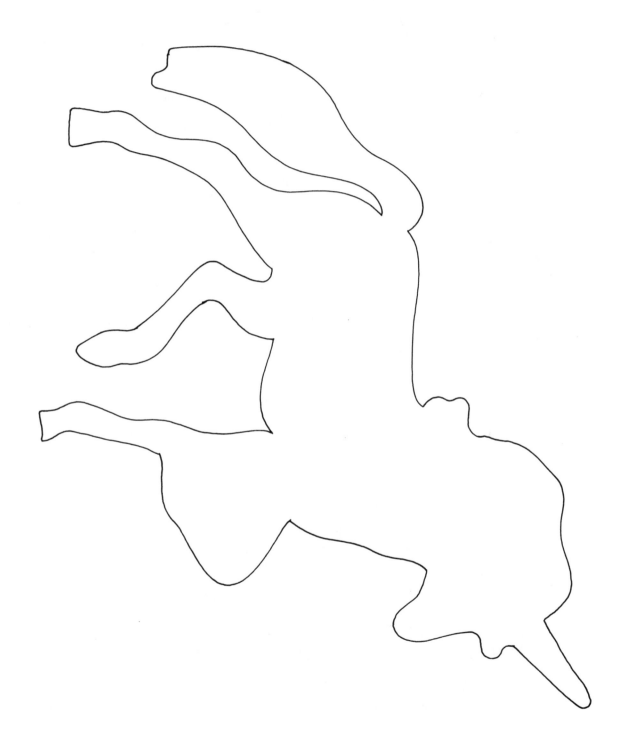

A47. VAN

A48. VEST

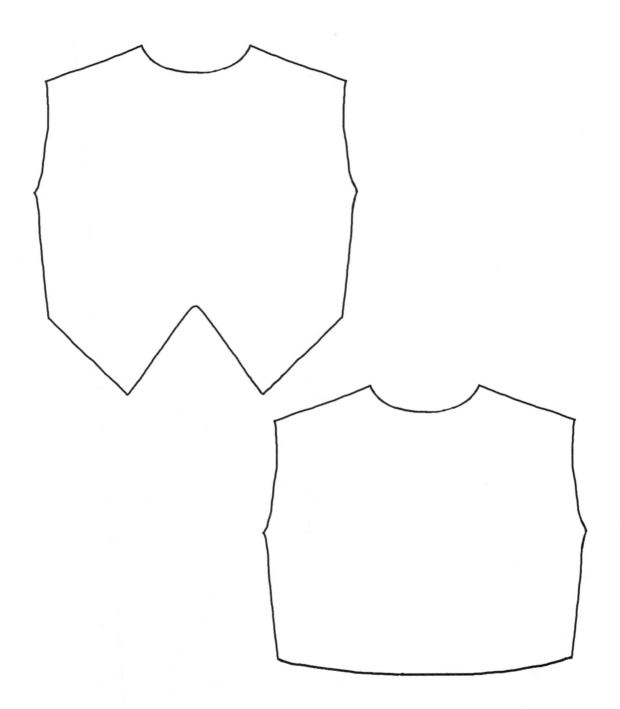

A49. WATERMELON SLICE

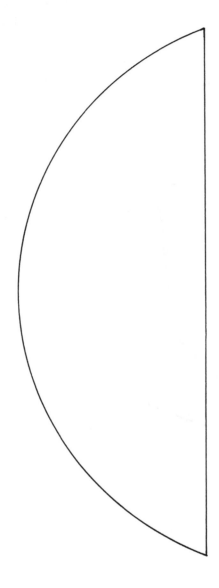

A50. WESTERN WAGON BASE AND COVER

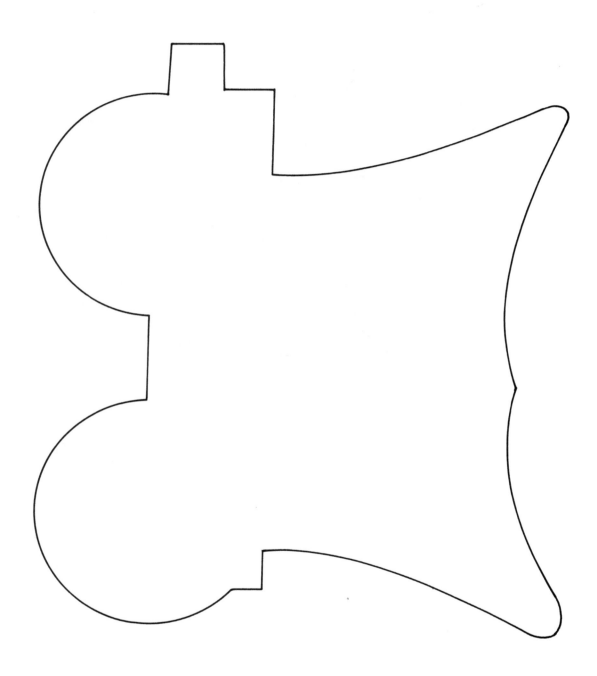

A51. ZEBRA

A52. ZINNIA AND STEM

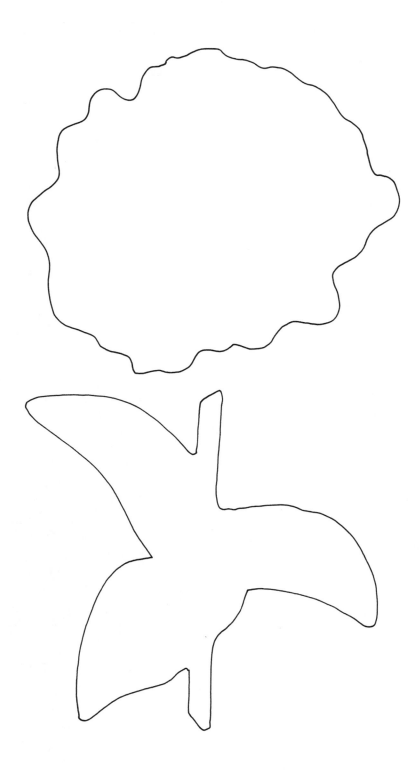

Index of Math Concepts

Index of Units

Index